GOD'S
PROMISES®
DEVOTIONAL
JOURNAL

January

The promises of God are dependable.
WARREN W. WIERSBE

January 1

The LORD is slow to anger and great in power.
NAHUM 1:3

God's power, one of His primary attributes, is often on display for our good. It supports us in our troubles and strengthens our spiritual life.

In His parting words to the disciples, just prior to His ascension, Jesus promised, "'But you shall receive power when the Holy Spirit has come upon you; and you shall be witnesses to Me in Jerusalem, and in all Judea and Samaria, and to the end of the earth'" (Acts 1:8).

Whether our outward circumstances are favorable or unfavorable, these and other divine promises about God's power are there for us to claim.

—JOHN MACARTHUR
Truth for Today

What is one way God has recently displayed His power in your life?

_____

_____

_____

_____

_____

_____

_____

_____

_____

_____

_____

January 2

He who keeps His commandments abides in Him, and He in him.
1 JOHN 3:24

Many things in your life will change over time. But thankfully, by God's grace, when the Holy Spirit enters the life of a believer, He's there to stay.

We learn from Jesus Himself (1 Corinthians 6:19) that God makes a believer's life a temple in which He dwells through His Spirit. That truth has profound implications for how we live. We are, for instance, to be good stewards of our body, which is the temple of God's Holy Spirit.

Even as God abides in a believer's life, we are to abide in Him. To abide in God is to live in His presence and, as a result, to take on His characteristics. His life becomes our life as our life is hidden in Him.

We are therefore to face every situation and relate to every person with the distinct awareness that Jesus is always with us *and* within us.

—HENRY AND RICHARD BLACKABY
Discovering God's Daily Agenda

How does knowing the truth that Jesus' Spirit dwells within you affect how you will live out your day today? and tomorrow?

January 3

In Your hand is power and might;
In Your hand it is to make great
And to give strength to all.
1 CHRONICLES 29:12

The crowning jewel of Creation was man himself. He was created for a distinct purpose. If the purpose is lived out, life is fulfilling. If the purpose is rejected or ignored, life will never be what it was meant to be.

Apart from the Creator's purpose, you and I are like a light bulb lying in a meaningless, useless state. We need to fit into the Creator's original design, plugging into the power source—our relationship with Him—if our lives are to be what they were meant to be.

—ANNE GRAHAM LOTZ
God's Story

Have you found your purpose in life? If so, what are you doing with it?

January 4

You cannot add any time
to your life by worrying about it.
MATTHEW 6:27 NCV

Anxiety is an expensive habit. Of course, it might be worth the cost if it worked. But it doesn't. Our frets are futile.

Worry has never brightened a day, solved a problem, or cured a disease.

God leads us. God will do the right thing at the right time. And what a difference that makes.

—MAX LUCADO
Traveling Light

What are three things that worry you the most? What can you do to help yourself become worry free?

January 5

If the Son makes you free,
you shall be free indeed.
JOHN 8:36

This freeing of the self is the real purpose of righteousness: the rightness that God asks of His children. Yet all too often we have thought that righteousness means the end of all our fun and freedom. Nothing could be further from the truth. God's love means sheer goodwill for us. Each of us can find the truth for ourselves only as we, step by step, walk the Faith Road, for God sees to it that sight never precedes faith.

—CATHERINE MARSHALL
Moments that Matter

Freedom is a gift from God. What are you doing to protect that freedom?

January 6

The Lord will open up his heavenly storehouse so that the skies send rain on your land at the right time, and he will bless everything you do.
DEUTERONOMY 28:12 NCV

The first belongs to God, and the principle of the firstfruits is very, very powerful. I have heard it said that any first thing given is never lost, and any first thing not given is always lost. In other words, what we give to God we don't lose because God redeems it for us. But what we withhold from God, we will lose. Jesus echoed this principle when He said, "For whoever wants to save their life will lose it, but whoever loses their life for me will find it" (Matthew 16:25 NIV).

Coming to church at the first of the week is a way of giving the Lord the first of your time. As God's people, we need to give the first part of our week to Jesus. The reason the New Testament church met on Sunday was because they were celebrating the resurrection of the Lord Jesus Christ. They gave the first of their time to God in worship.

—ROBERT MORRIS
The Blessed Life

Think of an example of how applying this principle would change how you prioritize your time.

_____

_____

_____

_____

_____

_____

January 7

A bruised reed he will not break, and a smoldering wick he will not snuff out.
ISAIAH 42:3 NIV

Your weakness and brokenness draw Me ever so near you. You can open up to Me because I understand you perfectly. My compassion for you is overflowing. As you open yourself to My healing Presence, I fill you with *Peace that transcends understanding.* So stop trying to figure everything out. Instead, lean on Me, letting your head rest on My chest. While you rest, I will be watching over you and all that concerns you.

Trust Me in the depths of your being, where I live in union with you. My healing work in you is most effective when you are actively trusting Me. *Though the mountains be shaken and the hills be removed, yet My unfailing Love for you will not be shaken.* This is the essence of My compassion for you: No matter how desperate your circumstances, the one thing you can always count on is *My unfailing Love.*

—SARAH YOUNG
Jesus Lives

What are some of the daily occurrences you "count on"? (Examples: The sun rising. The chair supporting your weight. Taking your next breath.) Knowing that all these things are possible because of the Lord, how can you cultivate a more active trust in His unfailing love?

January 8

As He who called you is holy,
you also be holy in all your conduct.
1 PETER 1:15

No human is holy in himself. Holiness is foreign to us. It is alien. That is why we require the righteousness of Another to cover our moral nakedness. The Holy One has given us the holiness we need in the cloak of Christ's righteousness.

—R. C. SPROUL
In the Presence of God

On a scale of 1–10, where are you in your Christian life? What do you have to change to be holy in all your conduct?

January 9

We can enter through a new and living way that Jesus opened
for us. It leads through the curtain—Christ's body.
HEBREWS 10:20 NCV

To the original readers, those last four words were explosive: "the curtain— Christ's body." According to the writer, the curtain equals Jesus. Hence, whatever happened to the flesh of Jesus happened to the curtain. What happened to His flesh? It was torn. Torn by the whips, torn by the thorns. Torn by the weight of the cross and the point of the nails. But in the horror of His torn flesh, we find the splendor of the open door. . . .

We are welcome to enter into God's presence—any day, any time.

—MAX LUCADO
He Chose the Nails

How can you make each promise God has given a part of your everyday life?

January 10

You are a chosen generation, a royal priesthood,
a holy nation, His own special people,
that you may proclaim the praises of Him who called
you out of darkness into His marvelous light.
1 PETER 2:9

Who are we in Jesus? Better yet, who are *you* in Jesus? Read the following truths slowly so that you hear them with your heart and not just your ears! In fact, trade every *you* for *I* and let the truth penetrate your heart anew! You are cleansed and forgiven (1 John 1:9); you are a new creation (2 Corinthians 5:17). You are loved by your heavenly Father and have been adopted as his child (1 John 3:1). You are fearfully and wonderfully made (Psalm 139:14), and God delights in you (Psalm 147:11). You are God's chosen (1 Peter 2:9); you are the apple of his eye (Psalm 17:8).

—SHEILA WALSH
Good Morning, Lord

What, if anything, keeps you from living with absolute confidence that God loves you
and from remembering who you are in Christ?

January 11

Because narrow is the gate and difficult is the way
which leads to life, and there are few who find it.
MATTHEW 7:14

G od makes it clear that the road to life is rough. You will begin every new adventure in life with naïve hope and excitement. Every wedding will begin with passion then move into problems. Every decorated nursery will receive a baby that will present unanticipated challenges. Everything you do, no matter how well organized and well intentioned, will run into trouble.

He also makes it clear that there isn't a better, more satisfying, less bumpy road through your life that will lead to real joy. The road to life will expose you to terrible failure and crushing conflict. But only *that* road leads to the life you want, the life that God gives.

—DR. LARRY CRABB
66 Love Letters

List some of the difficulties you are currently facing in life. Challenge yourself to walk the narrow road of belief that welcomes exposure of failure and conflict, knowing that God has a plan to overcome them.

January 12

So you shall serve the LORD your God,
and He will bless your bread and your water.
EXODUS 23:25

You may find temporary satisfaction in things and people, but permanent, deep, full satisfaction of your very being is only found in a right relationship with God for whom you were created.

Not only is your being created for God, but your doing is created for God also. You and I were created for commitment to serve God.

—ANNE GRAHAM LOTZ
God's Story

What are you presently involved in that will help you grow in your spiritual life?

January 13

Choose life, that both you and your descendants may live.
DEUTERONOMY 30:19

Some choices are easy . . . Paper or plastic? Regular or unleaded? For here or to go? Others take a lot more wisdom: Which job should I take? Where should I live? Whom should I marry? How can I be a better parent? What is a wise use of my finances?

Every day is filled with choices, both big and small. And God wants to help you make them wisely. He's already given you what you need: the wisdom and understanding included in the Bible—through precept and example—God's whisper in your heart, and the acquired wisdom of family and friends.

God's Daily Answer

Do you sometimes forget or neglect to ask God for wisdom and guidance when making an important decision?

_____

_____

_____

_____

_____

_____

_____

_____

_____

_____

_____

January 14

For I am the LORD, I do not change.
MALACHI 3:6 KJV

L ook upon a Christian in his spiritual estate, and he is full of variation. Sometimes his faith is at a high tide, sometimes low ebb. Sometimes his love flames, and at other times he is like fire in the embers, and he has lost his first love.

But God is without any shadow of turning. God's glory shines with a fixed brightness. In God, there is nothing that looks like a change, for better or worse—not better, because then He were not perfect; not worse, for then He would cease to be perfect. He is immutably holy, immutably good. There is no shadow of change in Him.

—THOMAS WATSON
A Body of Divinity

What situations in life have caused your faith to waver? What can you do to turn them into times of shining glory?

January 15

Let us hold fast the confession of our hope without wavering, for He who promised is faithful.
HEBREWS 10:23

If there's one thing most people don't like about the modern political process, it would have to be the abundance of promises candidates make, but often can't keep. After they are elected, the political process gets so complicated it becomes impossible for politicians to keep all their campaign promises. But promises are important—and not just in politics. We depend on the ability to trust one another's words in order to have meaningful relationships in life. The Bible tells us that God's words are wholly trustworthy—that they last forever. Whatever God says, whatever promises He makes, we know His words will never fail. An absolutely perfect promise keeper—that's the kind of God He is!

—DAVID JEREMIAH
1 Minute a Day

One part of trusting God is being patient and waiting on Him. Are you able to trust God wholeheartedly and wait on Him, or do you see God's Word as failed campaign promises that will never come to fruition?

January 16

From the rising of the sun to it's going down,
the LORD's name is to be praised.
PSALM 113:3

There is no schedule when it comes to giving thanks to God. You can thank Him in the morning when you pray to start your day. You can set your alarm to remind yourself to give Him thanks at lunchtime. And bedtime offers the opportunity to reflect on . . . and give thanks for . . . the blessings you might have taken for granted throughout the day.

But what about all those other minutes of the day? That moment when you looked out the window and saw the sunrise and the breathtaking beauty of the Lord filling the skies? Do you have to wait until noon to thank Him for this glorious display? Of course not. Or what about when you almost ran into the car that pulled out in front of you—but you didn't? Should you wait until you go to bed to thank God for giving you quick reflexes and good brakes? No way!

—KARLA DORNACHER
Give Thanks

Do you see every moment of the day as an opportunity to worship and give thanks to God? What are some of the more "normal" aspects of your daily life that could be chances to show your appreciation to God?

_____

_____

_____

_____

_____

January 17

It is to your advantage that I go away;
for if I do not go away, the Helper will not come to you;
but if I depart, I will send Him to you.

JOHN 16:7

When Jesus left this world He went to the Father. His ascension was to a certain place for a particular reason. To ascend did not mean merely "to go up." He was being elevated to the right hand of the Father. The seat He occupies on His departure is the royal throne of cosmic authority. It is the office of the King of kings and the Lord of lords.

—R. C. SPROUL
In the Presence of God

How much time do you spend each day listening to the Holy Spirit?

January 18

I will turn their mourning to joy,
Will comfort them,
And make them rejoice rather than sorrow.
JEREMIAH 31:13

Human beings by nature want to hug life and hold onto it, choke it down, save it and keep it. But Jesus taught there's only one way to know life's meaning: we gain happiness by letting go of this life. What is joy? It is Christ.

—CALVIN MILLER
Into the Depths of God

What area of your life do you need to let go so you can receive the joy God intended for you?

January 19

If you keep My commandments,
you will abide in my love.
JOHN 15:10

L earning to pray is learning to trust the wisdom, the power, and the love of our Heavenly Father, always so far beyond our dreams. He knows our need and knows ways to meet it that have never entered our heads. Things we feel sure we need for happiness may often lead to our ruin. Things we think will ruin us, . . . if we believe what the Father tells us and surrender ourselves into His strong arms, bring us deliverance and joy.

—ELISABETH ELLIOT
Keep a Quiet Heart

If there is anything in your life that is keeping you from experiencing all of God's love, ask His forgiveness today.

_____

_____

_____

_____

_____

_____

_____

_____

_____

_____

_____

January 20

It is no longer I who live,
but Christ lives in me.
GALATIANS 2:20

L ittle by little we are changed by this daily crucifixion of the will. Changed, not like a tornado changes things, but like a grain of sand in an oyster changes things. New graces emerge: new ability to cast all our care upon God, new joy at the success of others, new hope in a God who is good. . . . God is not destroying the will but transforming it so that over a process of time and experience we can freely will what God wills.

—RICHARD J. FOSTER
Prayer: Finding the Heart's True Home

What changes in your life will allow you to experience Christ living in you every day?

_____

_____

_____

_____

_____

_____

_____

_____

_____

_____

January 21

*You have filled my heart with
greater joy than when their grain
and new wine abound.*

PSALM 4:7 NIV

In David's time, the hope of many rested upon the outcome of the year's harvest. If the crops were plentiful, the community rejoiced. If the crops failed, the community despaired. But David experienced a joy that flourished even when crops perished. He treasured a joy that thrived even through drought. David knew a joy that was pure. Such joy flows from one source: the living God.

—ALICIA BRITT CHOLE
Pure Joy

List five blessings in your life that you can celebrate with friends.

_____

_____

_____

_____

_____

_____

_____

_____

_____

_____

January 22

*Do not be conformed to this world, but be transformed by the
renewing of your mind, that you may prove what is that
good and acceptable and perfect will of God.*

ROMANS 12:2

How long did it take for you to realize you do not know everything? When you come to the realization that there is still much for you to learn, you open the door to becoming a lifelong learner. In your Christian life, God reveals himself when you surrender to His Word and the leading of His Spirit. God does not simply want you to try harder or sin less, but also to depend on His Spirit and allow yourself to be transformed into someone who loves to please Him through willing obedience.

—JACK COUNTRYMAN
Time with God for Fathers

*Answer the question above. Then decide what steps you will take to become a lifelong
learner of God's Word.*

January 23

Do not grieve the Holy Spirit of God, by whom
you were sealed for the day of redemption.
EPHESIANS 4:30

If you are like I am, you love surprises. The greatest surprise you will ever experience is the surprising joy that comes when God, through His Holy Spirit, fills your heart to the fullest. Your days will be filled with more than you would ever ask or even dream of.

—NEIL CLARK WARREN
God Said It, Don't Sweat It

Is there any part of your life where you need to ask God for His help so as to not grieve the Holy Spirit?

_____

_____

_____

_____

_____

_____

_____

_____

_____

_____

_____

January 24

Far as the east is from the west,
So far has He removed our transgressions from us.
PSALM 103:12

Two big barriers exist in many Christians' lives: unforgiveness and guilt. Unforgiveness keeps us from being able to share what's good in our lives, and guilt causes us continual pain. I've met so many moms and dads who are unable to forgive their adult children for the pain they've caused them—and those parents are often wracked with guilt thinking they are somehow to blame for their children's problems. Sometimes these feeling are so entrenched there is no way humanly possible to get out of the pit they've created.

Only God can bring about changes in our hearts. As Psalm 103:8–14 reminds us, when we have wronged and disappointed Him, we ask forgiveness and He grants it. He removes our mistakes and guilt "as far as the east is from the west." Then He waits for us to do the same to those who have wronged and disappointed us.

—BARBARA JOHNSON
Women of Faith Devotional Bible

How does unforgiveness or guilt play a role in your relationships with your parents or your children?

Then I will say to those who were not My people, "You are my people!" And they shall say, "You are my God!"
HOSEA 2:23

The lack of self-esteem is the number-one emotional problem in America after depression. People are on a desperate search for self-significance. There is Someone who loves you enough that He sent His Son to the cross so you might have everlasting life. His arms are extended today saying, "The one who comes to Me I will be no means cast out" (John 6:37). You've never known the love of anything in your life until Jesus puts His arms around you and His love abides upon you.

—JOHN HAGEE
Life Lessons to Live By

Have you ever felt rejected, underappreciated, or unloved? Do you find comfort in the fact that Jesus loves you and would never reject or neglect you?

January 26

Pray without ceasing. . . . He who
calls you is faithful, who also will do it.
1 THESSALONIANS 5:17, 24

Jesus taught that answered prayer requires persistence. There may be a period when the door of blessing on which we hammer in prayer remains shut to us. Yet if we persist in knocking, the promise is that God will eventually open the door.

—CATHERINE MARSHALL
Moments that Matter

When you read the words, "Pray without ceasing," what does it mean to you and your prayer life?

January 27

Your testimonies are wonderful;
Therefore my soul keeps them.
PSALM 119:129

There are those who regard the Bible principally as the history of Israel. Others admit that it sets forth the soundest ethics ever enunciated. But these things, important as they are, are only incidental to the real theme of the Bible, which is the story of God's redemption as it exists in Jesus Christ.

Those who read the Scriptures as magnificent literature, breathtaking poetry or history, and overlook the story of salvation, miss the Bible's real meaning and message.

—BILLY GRAHAM
Peace with God

If someone were to ask you the question, "Why do you read the Bible?" what would you say?

___

___

___

___

___

___

___

___

___

___

January 28

*People may make plans in their minds, but the
LORD decides what they will do.*
PROVERBS 16:9 NCV

Sometimes, we must accept life on its terms, not our own. Life has a way of unfolding, not as *we* will, but as *it* will. And sometimes, there is precious little we can do to change things. When events transpire that are beyond our control, we have a choice: We can either learn the art of acceptance, or we can make ourselves miserable as we struggle to change the unchangeable.

We must entrust the things we *cannot* change to God. Once we have done so, we can prayerfully and faithfully tackle the important work that He has placed before us: the things we *can* change.

—CRISWELL FREEMAN
Purpose for Everyday Living

When in your life have you tried to change what was unchangeable? What was the final outcome of that situation?

January 29

God is able to make all grace abound toward you,
that you . . . may have an abundance for every good work.
2 CORINTHIANS 9:8

I'm so grateful Jesus enables me to change, one groaning effort at a time, and I'm thankful for those folks in my life who have given me the space and time to change. It's easy (but not loving) to view a person in one light and mentally lock that person into never being different.

Grace is a liberating quality—no, let me restate that. Grace is a required quality for family members, mates, moms, servants, and friends. Grace is a wide space, acreage full of forgiveness, humility, acceptance, safety, and love. When I consider what great things the Lord has done for me, grace and friendships make me want to break out bags of confetti, kazoos, and my most outrageous party hat!

—PATSY CLAIRMONT
The Hat Box

What does God's abundant grace mean to you? How do you extend this grace toward others?

January 30

In the beginning was the Word.

JOHN 1:1

In 700 BC, the conventional wisdom was that the earth was flat. Not only did the common man think it was flat, but the intellectuals were also convinced of this.

Yet even though all mankind was convinced of the flatness of the earth, note this verse from Isaiah 40:22: "It is He who sits above the circle of the earth." The word *circle* would have never been used if a mortal had written that book unassisted. But God inspired the man who wrote it, ensuring that the Bible was correct in its terminology.

The Bible will always withstand scientific challenges. In fact, not only has science never proven any part of the Bible wrong, over time, it has a way of actually proving it to be right.

—BRYANT WRIGHT
Right from the Heart

How does knowing the Bible was inspired by God deepen your faith and belief that His Word is truth?

January 31

In all their distress, he too was distressed, . . .
he lifted them up and carried them.
ISAIAH 63:9 NIV

The solution to loneliness is not to give in or give up or do what everyone else does or go where everyone else goes or look like and speak like and think like and act like the world around you so you won't stand out so sharply from the crowd. The solution is not to withdraw into an uninvolved, inactive life.

The solution is found when we discover meaning in the midst of loneliness as God Himself shares our loneliness while we walk with and work for Him.

—ANNE GRAHAM LOTZ
God's Story

Everyone faces a certain degree of loneliness. What did you do during this time in your life?

_____

_____

_____

_____

_____

_____

_____

_____

_____

February

*Our faith is not based on speculation
but upon God and His Word.*
BILLY GRAHAM

February 1

This also comes from the LORD of hosts,
Who is wonderful in counsel and excellent in guidance.
ISAIAH 28:29

The most direct way we see the goodness of God's wisdom is when He shares it with us. The apostle Paul prayed that He would grant to believers in Ephesus and everywhere "the spirit of wisdom and revelation in the knowledge of Him" (Ephesians 1:17). He expressed similar sentiments in his letter to the Colossians: "Let the word of Christ dwell in you richly in all wisdom, teaching and admonishing one another in psalms and hymns and spiritual songs, singing with grace in your hearts to the Lord" (3:16).

—JOHN MACARTHUR
Truth for Today

Choose a verse from God's Word to dwell in your heart and mind today. Write it down and explain how it helps you to see His goodness.

_____

_____

_____

_____

_____

_____

_____

_____

_____

February 2

Faith comes by hearing,
and hearing by the word of God.
ROMANS 10:17

Why would Bible reading produce faith? Certainly not because there is something magical about the book. The real reasons are far more direct . . . : (1) We can scarcely claim God's promises for ourselves until we know what He has promised. (2) The Bible is a series of true stories of God's dealing with men and women quite like us.

There are pioneers, adventurers, and businessmen. . . . When we read this book intelligently, we learn how God deals with humankind, what He is like, and what we can expect from Him.

—CATHERINE MARSHALL
Moments that Matter

How much time do you spend reading the Bible? Are there some habits you need to change?

February 3

Casting all your care upon Him,
for He cares for you.
1 PETER 5:7

To know God, or even to begin to know Him, is to know that we are not alone in the universe. Someone Else is Out There. There is a hint that there may be a refuge for our loneliness. To stop our frantic getting, spending, and searching, and simply to look at the things God has made is to move one step away from despair, for God cares. The most awesome seascape can reveal a care that is actually tender.

—ELISABETH ELLIOT
Keep a Quiet Heart

How can you arrange your daily life to allow Him into your lifestyle?

_____

_____

_____

_____

_____

_____

_____

_____

_____

_____

February 4

It is God who works in you both
to will and to do for His good pleasure.
PHILIPPIANS 2:13

The only purpose or intention God ever has is altogether good. When the Bible speaks of the sovereign exercise of the pleasure of His will, there is no hint of arbitrariness or wicked intent. The pleasure of His will is always the good pleasure of His will. His pleasure is always good; His will is always good; His intentions are always good.

—R. C. SPROUL
In the Presence of God

How can you experience God's pleasure and His perfect will?

February 5

And you shall tell your son in that day, saying, "This is done because of what the Lord did for me when I came up from Egypt."
EXODUS 13:8

Knowing your Christian heritage can strengthen your trust in and devotion to God. The Israelites were to tell the next generation about the powerful works God did in delivering them from slavery in Egypt—the plagues, the angel of death, the parting of the Red Sea, and the destruction of the Egyptian army. Likewise, we are to tell the next generation about the wonders God did in delivering us from slavery to sin—Christ coming in human form, living a sinless life, His willingness to submit to death on a cross, the brutal crucifixion, and the glorious resurrection.

—HENRY AND RICHARD BLACKABY
Discovering God's Daily Agenda

What is your faith story? At what moments has God's grace been unmistakably at work in your life?

February 6

Honor the Lord with your possessions,
And with the firstfruits of all your increase;
So your barns will be filled with plenty,
And your vats will overflow with new wine.
PROVERBS 3:9–10

God's Word makes it clear that we are to honor the Lord with the first-fruits of all of our increase. When we do, according to the verse above, our "barns will be filled with plenty, and [our] vats will overflow."

Unfortunately, the reason churches have so many special offerings is that only 1.7 percent of our income is being given to God.

Imagine what God's people could accomplish on earth if His people faith-fully gave Him the first 10 percent of their increase so that the remaining 90 percent is redeemed and blessed! Imagine the plans and purposes of God that could be advanced in this world if the Church would wake up to the blessings that come as a result of having the faith to give the firstfruits!

—ROBERT MORRIS
The Blessed Life

In what ways has Satan used fear to keep you from being financially faithful? What can you do so that faith in God's promises will overcome?

_____

_____

_____

_____

_____

_____

February 7

*I will heal them and reveal
to them the abundance of peace and truth.*
JEREMIAH 33:6

God caused the Bible to be written for the express purpose of revealing to man God's plan for redemption. God caused this Book to be written that He might make His everlasting laws clear to His children, and that they might have His great wisdom to guide them and His great love to comfort them as they make their way through life. For without the Bible, this world would indeed be a dark and frightening place, without signpost or beacon.

—BILLY GRAHAM
Peace with God

Does spending time in God's Word help you understand the abundance of peace and truth from the Bible?

February 8

But as for me, I watch in hope for the LORD,
I wait for God my Savior; my God will hear me.
MICAH 7:7 NIV

When you feel unable to pray, remember that the Spirit Himself intercedes for you with groans that words cannot express. Some of your prayers that you consider frantic and unintelligible are actually quite profound. They rise from the depths of your heart—all the way to heaven. To form these deep prayers, you need only turn toward Me with the concerns that lie heavy on your heart.

I want you to *watch in hope* as you *wait for Me, your Savior.* Wait expectantly: confident that I will do what is best. The longer you have to wait, the more you must rely on your trust in Me. If you start to feel anxious, seek My help with short prayers such as "Jesus, fill me with Your Peace." You may breathe these brief prayers as often as needed. As you put your hope in Me, *My unfailing Love rests peacefully upon you.*

—SARAH YOUNG
Jesus Lives

What concerns are pressing in on you right now? Write them here and then share them out loud with the Lord, remembering that you are talking with your closest Friend.

February 9

You will keep in perfect peace
all who trust in you,
all whose thoughts are fixed on you!
Trust in the LORD always,
for the LORD GOD is the eternal Rock.
ISAIAH 26:3–4 NLT

Perfect peace is translated from the Hebrew *shalom shalom*, which means "fulfillment, abundance, well-being, security." The phrase *whose mind is stayed on You* comes from two Hebrew words: the first meaning "will, imagination"; the second, "dependent, supported, firm." When our wills and imaginations are dependent on God, when we choose to turn our thoughts to him, we learn the simple truth that God is enough. We find out, as Isaiah wrote, that "in the Lord . . . is everlasting strength" (26:4), and in God's strength we discover fulfillment and security.

—SHEILA WALSH
Good Morning, Lord

When, if ever, have you experienced for yourself the simple and soul-satisfying truth that God is enough? Why don't we believers experience that more regularly?

_____

_____

_____

_____

_____

_____

_____

February 10

Therefore whoever hears these sayings of Mine, and does them,
I will liken him to a wise man who built his house on the rock . . . But
everyone who hears these sayings of Mine, and does not do them,
will be like a foolish man who built his house on the sand.
MATTHEW 7:24, 26

God teaches us two lessons from David's adulterous relationship with Bath-sheba: one, great men sin greatly, as all people do, so be alert; and two, when things are going well as they were for David, it's tempting to relax your guard and indulge your desires. David should have been leading his army. Instead, he stayed home, seduced a soldier's wife, and then had that soldier killed to keep it a secret so he could continue in a comfortable lifestyle.

For a short season (and more than once), David valued a comfortable life above a holy life and built his house on sand.

—DR. LARRY CRABB
66 Love Letters

Be honest, do you sometimes value immediate and shallow pleasures available now over permanent and deep pleasures available later?

February 11

The LORD is good;
His mercy is everlasting,
And His truth endures to all generations.
PSALM 100:5

Truth is timeless. Truth does not differ from one age to another, from one people to another, from one geographical location to another. Men's ideas may differ, men's customs may change, men's moral codes may vary, but God's great all-prevailing Truth stands for time and eternity.

—BILLY GRAHAM
Peace with God

How important is it for you to explore and find God's truth in the Bible?

_____

_____

_____

_____

_____

_____

_____

_____

_____

_____

_____

_____

_____

February 12

The LORD is their strength,
And He is the saving refuge of His anointed.
PSALM 28:8

Once we give ourselves up to God, shall we attempt to get hold of what can never belong to us—tomorrow? Our lives are His, our times and in His hand. He is Lord over what will happen, never mind what may happen. When we prayed "Thy will be done," did we suppose He did not hear us? He heard indeed, and daily makes our business His. If my life is once surrendered, all is well. Let me not grab it back, as though it were in peril in His hand but would be safer in mine!

—ELISABETH ELLIOT
Keep a Quiet Heart

What does it mean for you to surrender your life to Jesus Christ?

February 13

Humble yourselves before the Lord, and he will lift you up.
JAMES 4:10 NIV

You are God's priceless treasure—unique in beauty, design, and potential. There are accomplishments and victories you have achieved that you can be proud of. God is certainly proud of the person you've become. But, if you look closely, you almost certainly will have to admit that everything you are and everything you've done can be traced back to God.

That's why humility is more than a positive character trait—it's a paradox. It's holding in one hand how much you've achieved and in the other how deeply dependent you are on the One who has helped you achieve it.

God's Daily Answer

When you receive praise from others, do you pause for a moment to put everything into perspective and humble yourself before the Lord?

February 14

The Lord seeth not as man seeth; for man looketh on the outward appearance, but the Lord looketh on the heart.
1 SAMUEL 16:7 KJV

Men judge the heart by the actions. God judges the actions by the heart. If the heart be sincere, God will see the faith and bear with the failing. Sincerity makes our duties acceptable, like musk among linen that perfumes it. As Jehu said to Jehonadab in 2 Kings 10:15, "Is thine heart right . . . ? And Jehonadab said, It is. If it be, give me thine hand. And he gave him his hand; and he took him up into the chariot." If God sees our heart is right—that we love Him and desire His glory—says He, give Me your prayers and tears; now you shall come up with Me into the chariot of glory.

Sincerity makes our services to be golden, and God will not cast away the gold. . . .

—THOMAS WATSON
A Body of Divinity

Is your heart right with God today? If not, what do you need to do to make it right?

February 15

He who has begun a good work in you
will complete it until the day of Jesus Christ.
PHILIPPIANS 1:6

God is looking for those who believe that what He says is more important than what anyone else says. That what He thinks is more important than what anyone else thinks. That what He wants is more important than what anyone else wants. That His will is more important than their own.

God is looking for another Noah. Another Meshach. Another Shadrach. Another Abednego.

One person with God is not alone but a majority!

—ANNE GRAHAM LOTZ
God's Story

How important is God's Word and what He says to your Christian walk?

_____

_____

_____

_____

_____

_____

_____

_____

_____

_____

_____

February 16

The law of the LORD is perfect,
converting the soul;
The testimony of the LORD is sure,
making wise the simple.
PSALM 19:7

Albert Einstein, the famous physicist, explained relativity this way: When a man sits with a pretty girl for an hour, it seems like a minute. But when he sits on a hot stove for a minute, it seems like an hour. That's relativity, he said. Lots of things in life are relative—they change when compared to something else. But one thing that is not relative is God's truth found in the Bible. The words of Scripture were true when they were written, are true today, and will be true when we're long gone. We can safely build our lives on the unchanging foundation of Scripture. If you're looking for unfailing truth, look in God's Word.

—DAVID JEREMIAH
1 Minute a Day

Where else do you look in your search for truth? Truth may be found in our own
scientific and philosophical knowledge of the universe, but that may change, just as it
has changed throughout history. So why not look to the unchanging God for truth?

February 17

God is greater than our heart,
and knows all things.
1 JOHN 3:20

You and I are governed. The weather determines what we wear. The terrain tells us how to travel. Gravity dictates our speed, and health determines our strength. We may challenge these forces and alter them slightly, but we never remove them.

God—our Shepherd—doesn't check the weather; He makes it. He doesn't defy gravity; He created it.

God is what He is. What He has always been. God is Yahweh—an unchanging God, an uncaused God, and an ungoverned God.

—MAX LUCADO
Traveling Light

If God is in charge and knows all things, what is your purpose in the world today?

_____

_____

_____

_____

_____

_____

_____

_____

_____

_____

February 18

Therefore, if anyone is in Christ, he is a new creation; old things
have passed away; behold, all things have become new.
2 CORINTHIANS 5:17

I love taking an old piece of furniture and giving it new life by stripping off the old paint and replacing it with a fresh, clean coat of color. It makes my heart glad to save something that was headed for the trash and give it a second chance.

The Bible tells us that we are new creations in Christ. Just as the butterfly looks nothing like the lowly worm it once was, so it is with us: the old is gone and all things have become new. But God didn't use sandpaper and paint. He used the death and resurrection of Jesus. Unconditional love. Undeserved favor.

I'm sure if that table could talk, it would say, "Thank you." I know I would—or would I? After a few weeks of settling into daily life and having the compliments dwindle, would I begin to take my new life for granted? After receiving a few watermarks from careless glasses and being used as a resting place for dishes and dirty feet, would I become discontent with this new life? Would I forget about my salvation from the trash heap?

—KARLA DORNACHER
Give Thanks

Does the routine of everyday life sometimes cause you to forget that God, in His infinite mercy, has saved you from the trash heap of eternal death and destruction?

_____

_____

_____

_____

February 19

You are my lamp, O Lord;
The Lord shall enlighten my darkness.
2 SAMUEL 22:29

Knowledge of the Bible is essential to a rich and meaningful life, for the words of this Book have a way of filling in the missing pieces, of bridging the gaps, of turning the tarnished colors of our life to jewel-like brilliance. Learn to take your every problem to the Bible. Within its pages you will find the correct answer.

—BILLY GRAHAM
Peace with God

How much time do you spend reading your Bible? How does your devotional time with God change the way you look at life?

February 20

How much better to get wisdom than gold!
And to get understanding is to be chosen rather than silver.
PROVERBS 16:16

The love of money touches everyone in life, and we often spend most of our working hours trying to get more. The more we get, the more we want. Our appetite is for material possessions we do not necessarily need. The Bible condemns the desire to get rich, not because money is a sin, but because money makes a terrible master. People whose primary goal is to get rich serve money—and therefore cannot serve God.

—JACK COUNTRYMAN
Time with God for Fathers

How much time do you spend earning money? In your list of priorities, where does God fall compared to money?

_____

_____

_____

_____

_____

_____

_____

_____

_____

_____

_____

February 21

A man's heart plans his way,
But the LORD directs his steps.
PROVERBS 16:9

There are two things I might've changed about my life: I wouldn't have been the youngest in a family of eight (although I can't decide which sibling I could live without!), and I wouldn't have grown up poor.

But we don't always know what we might need in life. There are many positive aspects of my adult life that I can directly attribute to growing up in my family of origin, in our tiny little town.

Because I was little, I learned to speak up. Because I was young, I learned to keep up. And because I was last, I learned to make up the difference. All of that has served me well through the years. When I'm in over my head, I'm comfortable reaching. When I'm overwhelmed, I keep going. When I'm overcommitted, I hang on. Just like my siblings did. God has His purpose for everything.

—MARY GRAHAM
Women of Faith Devotional Bible

What is one thing you might have wanted to change about your life? How has God used it for your good now?

_____

_____

_____

_____

_____

_____

February 22

He who heeds the word wisely will find good,
And whoever trusts in the LORD, happy is he.
PROVERBS 16:20

When you find yourself drowning in overwhelming circumstances, ask God to give you a promise to which you can cling—a promise on which you can base your hope. Hope that is based simply on what you want or what you feel is not a genuine expression of faith.

Our hope must be based on God's Word.

—ANNE GRAHAM LOTZ
God's Story

What promise from God's Word can you cling to today?

February 23

He makes me to lie down in green pastures;
He leads me beside the still waters.
PSALM 23:2

Note the two pronouns preceding the two verbs. *He* makes me . . . *He* leads me . . .

Who is in charge? The Shepherd. The Shepherd selects the trail and prepares the pasture. The sheep's job—our job—is to watch the Shepherd.

—MAX LUCADO
Traveling Light

Who is your shepherd? To whom do you turn when stress comes into your life?

_____

_____

_____

_____

_____

_____

_____

_____

_____

_____

_____

_____

February 24

Therefore, having been justified by faith, we have peace
with God through our Lord Jesus Christ.
ROMANS 5:1

Where is peace found? Peace is not having an untroubled life. Peace is not found in a pill, in a bottle, in wealth, or in power. It is found in reconciliation with God. There can be no peace of mind until you surrender your life at the Cross.

When Jesus came to His disciples, He said, "My peace I give to you; not as the world gives do I give to you" (John 14:27). The peace of Christ is greater than the storm, the burden, the risk, or any responsibility we can face. It surpasses all understanding (Philippians 4:7), and you can have it if you want it!

—JOHN HAGEE
Life Lessons to Live By

Do you toss and turn on your bed at night? Do you have any unconfessed sin you're
holding on to?

February 25

I will wait for the God of my salvation;
My God will hear me.
MICAH 7:7

Even in the Garden of Gethsemane on the night of betrayal, Christ had plenty of time and opportunity to flee. But He would not flee. Instead He knelt to pray in the shadowy Garden under the gray-green leaves of the olive tress. And in His prayer that night, Jesus gave us, for all time, the perfect pattern for the Prayer of Relinquishment: "Not what I want, but what You want." . . . Jesus deliberately set himself to make His will and God's will the same.

—CATHERINE MARSHALL
Moments that Matter

Who is number one in your life? Are you willing to make God's will and your will the same?

February 26

Your thoughts toward us
Cannot be recounted to You in order;
If I would declare and speak of them,
They are more than can be numbered.
PSALM 40:5

As a watch must have a designer, so our precision-like universe has a Great Designer. We call Him God. His is a name with which we are familiar. From earliest childhood we have breathed His name. The Bible declares that the God we talk about, the God we sing about, the God "from whom all blessings flow!" is the God who created this world and placed us in it.

—BILLY GRAHAM
Peace with God

When you think about creation, what thoughts and questions come to mind that you would like to ask God?

February 27

So then faith comes by hearing, and hearing by the word of God.
ROMANS 10:17

Confidence means "living with faith," and faith is not inherited, it's developed. It is constantly in the process of developing. The Word of God is saturated with divine confidence. You can read the Bible and it will take your dull, doubting life and transform you into a fireball of divine action. In this sacred book you will meet men and women just like you who fall against impossible odds and win. With faith in God and faith in themselves, they faced giants, delivered millions of slaves from Egyptian bondage, called down fire from heaven, and healed the sick and raised the dead. Nothing is impossible to those who believe and are called according to the purpose of God!

—JOHN HAGEE
Life Lessons to Live By

Are you encouraged by the stories of God working through people who had great faith? Does it motivate you to develop your own faith?

February 28

Those who wait for perfect weather will never plant seeds; . . . Plant early in the morning, and work until evening, because you don't know if this or that will succeed. They might both do well.
ECCLESIASTES 11:4, 6 NCV

Once the season for planting is upon us, the time to plant seeds is when we *make* time to plant seeds. And when it comes to planting *God's* seeds in the soil of eternity, the only certain time that we have is now. Yet, because we are fallible human beings with limited vision and misplaced priorities, we may be tempted to delay.

If we hope to reap a bountiful harvest for God, our families, and for ourselves, we must plant *now* by defeating a dreaded human frailty: the habit of procrastination. Procrastination often results from our shortsighted attempts to postpone temporary discomfort. A far better strategy is this: Whatever "it" is, do it now. When you do, you won't have to worry about "it" later.

—CRISWELL FREEMAN
Purpose for Everyday Living

What have you been putting off that needs to be taken care of today? How are you going to get the job done?

March

A strong faith leads to a good attitude.
CHARLES R. SWINDOLL

March 1

Godliness with contentment is great gain.
1 TIMOTHY 6:6

When we surrender to God the cumbersome sack of discontent, we don't just give up something; we gain something. God replaces it with a lightweight, tailor-made, sorrow-resistant attaché of gratitude.

What will you gain with contentment? You may gain your marriage. You may gain precious hours with your children. You may gain your self-respect. You may gain joy.

—MAX LUCADO
Traveling Light

How is your contentment barometer? What do you need to do to have the peace that passes all understanding?

_____

_____

_____

_____

_____

_____

_____

_____

_____

_____

March 2

You are a chosen generation,
a royal priesthood . . . the people of God.
1 PETER 2:9–10

Several images are used in the Bible to describe the Church: the Body of Christ, the elect, the house of God, the saints. One of the most meaningful expressions the Bible uses is "the people of God," the *laos theon*.

The Church is not a building; it is not the clergy; it is not an abstract institution—it is the people of God.

—R. C. SPROUL
In the Presence of God

What steps are you taking to be used by God in the body of Christ?

March 3

There is therefore now no condemnation to those who are in Christ Jesus, who do not walk according to the flesh, but according to the Spirit.
ROMANS 8:1

No condemnation? None? Zip? Zilch? Wow! What a huge truth to get our arms around! Human nature is full of condemnation. I still remember the looks some adults gave me even as a kid. At times I wasn't sure what I had done, but I felt their piercing disapproval.

As an adult, when I find myself severe in my thoughts toward others who have offended me, I remember Romans 8. Christ freed me from all condemnation when He paid for my failures, mistakes, and bone-deep naughtiness, and His forgiveness offers me the grace and liberty to forgive others. Whew!

—PATSY CLAIRMONT
Women of Faith Devotional Bible

Write Romans 8:1 below and commit it to memory. And the next time you feel condemned (by anyone), quote the verse and claim God's promise for yourself!

_____

_____

_____

_____

_____

_____

_____

March 4

Look at the birds of the air, for they neither sow nor reap
nor gather into barns; yet your heavenly Father feeds
them. Are you not of more value than they?
MATTHEW 6:26

One morning I walked outside of our house as the light was just beginning to show on the horizon. The birds around our yard were chirping and singing. They were pumped about another day, getting ready to go to work, finding twigs for their nests and worms to chew on. They lived a lifestyle that shows a trust for their Creator while they go about gathering the resources He makes available to them.

But while the birds trust God day by day, they also work hard from dawn to dusk. As that famous philosopher, Anonymous, once said, "Pray as if everything depends on God, and then work as if everything depends on you." Pray to the Lord. Share with Him your worries and concerns. And then work hard like the birds. They just don't have time to worry. Neither do we when we trust God and work hard.

—BRYANT WRIGHT
Right from the Heart

What can you do differently to show more trust in your Creator? In what areas of life
can you worry less and work harder?

March 5

Every word of God is pure;
He is a shield to those who put their trust in Him.
PROVERBS 30:5

God has not changed. If He was faithful to watch over Noah and all those within the ark, bringing them safely through the storm, He will do the same for you. Just as He was faithful to preserve Joseph through thirteen years of slavery in Potiphar's house and Pharaoh's prison, just as He was faithful to preserve the little baby Moses floating on the Nile . . . God will be faithful to you.

—ANNE GRAHAM LOTZ
God's Story

What do you need to do to be faithful to God and those you care about?

March 6

Through the Lord's mercies we are not consumed,
Because His compassions fail not.
They are new every morning;
Great is Your faithfulness.
LAMENTATIONS 3:22–23

The goodness of God's faithfulness to believers is apparent, because even when we are unfaithful to Him, He remains faithful to us.

Whenever you're in need, you can rely on the faithfulness of God's promises, such as these: "He shall call upon Me, and I will answer him; I will be with him in trouble; I will deliver him and honor him" (Psalm 91:15); "And my God shall supply all your needs according to His riches in glory by Christ Jesus" (Philippians 4:19).

—JOHN MACARTHUR
Truth for Today

Write about a time when you have called on God and He showed Himself faithful.
End with a short prayer of praise and thanksgiving.

March 7

God's business is putting things right;
he loves getting the lines straight.
PSALM 11:7 MSG

In the wilderness of loneliness we are terribly vulnerable. What we want is OUT, and sometimes there appear to be some easy ways to get there. Will we take Satan up on his offers, satisfy our desires in ways never designed by God, seek security outside of His holy will? If we do, we may find a measure of happiness, but not the lasting joy our heavenly Father wants us to have.

—ELISABETH ELLIOT
Keep a Quiet Heart

So many things go on in our lives that keep us from putting things right. What changes can you make to get your life straight with God?

_____

_____

_____

_____

_____

_____

_____

_____

_____

_____

_____

March 8

Walk in love, as Christ also has
loved us and given Himself for us.
EPHESIANS 5:2

Do you love others? Do you love others as you love yourself? If so, you are undoubtedly in a right relationship with God! But if you find yourself focusing all of your attention on your own life exclusive of others, you can know for a fact that you haven't loved yourself the way you need to. All the love you need is totally available to you right now! God is ready to love you so powerfully that your love for others will become automatic and natural.

—NEIL CLARK WARREN
God Said It, Don't Sweat It

Who is most important in your love life? Yourself or others? Explain.

March 9

*This is the victory that has
overcome the world—our faith.*
1 JOHN 5:4

There is a difference between acceptance and resignation.
Resignation is barren of faith in the love of God. It says, "Grievous circumstances have come to me. There is no escaping them."

Acceptance says, "I trust the goodwill, the love of my God. I'll open my arms and my understanding to what He has allowed to come to me." Thus acceptance leaves the door of hope wide open to God's creative plan.

—CATHERINE MARSHALL
Moments that Matter

How hard is it to accept your circumstances yet live for God anyway?

March 10

God is right in everything he does.
DANIEL 9:14 NCV

God is never wrong. He has never rendered a wrong decision, experienced the wrong attitude, taken the wrong path, said the wrong thing, or acted the wrong way. He is never too late or too early, too loud or too soft, too fast or too slow. He has always been and always will be right. He is righteous.

—MAX LUCADO
Traveling Light

Have you ever questioned God about things that have happened in your life that you cannot control? How did you overcome your bewilderment?

March 11

He who believes in the Son of God
has the witness in himself.
1 JOHN 5:10

Man's only salvation from sin stands on a lonely, barren, skull-shaped hill; a thief hangs on one cross, a murderer on another, and between them, a Man with a crown of thorns. Blood flows from His hands and feet, it pours from His side, it drops down His face—while those who stand looking on sneer and mock.

Who is this tortured figure, this Man whom other men seek to humiliate and kill? He is the Son of God, the Prince of Peace.

—BILLY GRAHAM
Peace with God

We are called to be God's witnesses. What plans have you made to share your relationship with God?

_____

_____

_____

_____

_____

_____

_____

_____

_____

March 12

The God of peace will be with you.
PHILIPPIANS 4:9

The apostle Paul often referred to the Lord as the God of peace. In Romans he said, "Now the God of peace be with you all" (15:33). In 2 Corinthians he wrote, "The God of love and peace will be with you" (13:11).

God's character is peace. He is the origin and giver of peace. When we have godly attitudes, thoughts, and actions, the peace of God and the God of peace will guard us. His peace provides comfort, tranquility, quietness, and confidence in the midst of any trial you may face.

—JOHN MACARTHUR
Truth for Today

Is there any part of your life that feels unsettled and lacks God's peace? Write Isaiah 26:3 below and pray for His peace to reign in your heart.

March 13

Walk in the Spirit, and you shall not fulfill the lust of the flesh.
GALATIANS 5:16

Walking in the Spirit is a choice we make. It involves choosing—moment by moment—to live under the direction and in the power of the Holy Spirit.

Walking in the flesh will always produce sin. Walking in the Spirit will always result in righteousness. Life situations are opportunities for the Spirit residing in Christians to live out His life through them and to reveal to a watching world what God is like.

—HENRY AND RICHARD BLACKABY
Discovering God's Daily Agenda

Think of a time when you have experienced the power of the Holy Spirit working through you and the blessing you received. Write a prayer of commitment to "walk in the Spirit," and consider memorizing it and praying it at the beginning of each day.

March 14

*Christ died for sins once for all, the righteous for
the unrighteous, to bring you to God.*
1 PETER 3:18 NIV

The path of righteousness is a narrow, winding trail up a steep hill. At the top of the hill is a cross. At the base of the cross are bags. Countless bags full of innumerable sins. Calvary is the compost pile of guilt. Would you like to leave yours there as well?

—MAX LUCADO
Traveling Light

List the sins you need to release to God today. Then pray and ask for His forgiveness.

March 15

*The wages of sin is death, but the gift of God is
eternal life in Christ Jesus our Lord.*
ROMANS 6:23

The cross, sin's masterpiece of shame and hate, became God's masterpiece of mercy and forgiveness. Through the death of Christ upon the
cross, sin itself was crucified for those who believe in Him. Sin was con-
quered on the cross. His death is the foundation of our hope, the promise
of our triumph!

—BILLY GRAHAM
Peace with God

What does Jesus Christ's sacrifice on the cross mean to you?

March 16

And this stone which I have set as a pillar shall be God's house,
and of all that You give me I will surely give a tenth to You.
GENESIS 28:22

In the verse above we see that Jacob's vow to tithe came straight from his grateful heart. True tithing comes from the heart—not from a legalistic mind. Like his grandfather Abraham, Jacob wanted to give God the first of his firstfruits—the first 10 percent. Having experienced the sweetness of God's presence and goodness of His favor, Jacob wanted to bless Him. It was a heart thing.

True tithing from the heart does not leave you resentful or needy—it leaves you surrounded in the abundance of blessing, joy, and satisfaction that no other source can provide. That's why tithing is life to me, not law. And when tithing becomes life to you, it will be one of the greatest joys of your life.

—ROBERT MORRIS
The Blessed Life

Does the standard of giving that you practice meet, exceed, or fall short of the
principle of tithing?

March 17

The heavens are Yours, the earth also is Yours; . . .
You have a mighty arm;
Strong is Your hand.
PSALM 89:11, 13

As you and I see the winter snows give way to spring flowers and the summer's heat give way to autumn's briskness, we are reminded that in back of the changes is the God who never changes. The sun that always rises every morning and always sets every evening, the stars that always come out in the night sky, and the moon that always goes through its monthly phases—all reveal the glory of God, who is good!

—ANNE GRAHAM LOTZ
God's Story

What season of your spiritual life are you experiencing today?

_____

_____

_____

_____

_____

_____

_____

_____

_____

_____

_____

March 18

The LORD is near to all who call on him,
to all who call on him in truth.

PSALM 145:18

Nothing can separate you from My Love. When you trusted Me as Savior, I united Myself to you in eternal matrimony. Many things threaten to rip apart this holy bond—principalities and powers, controlling people, dire circumstances—but nothing can succeed, not even death. In fact, dying opens the way to ecstatic enjoyment of Me: exponentially better than your best moment on earth!

I embody not only perfect Love but *all the fullness of the Deity* as well. In Me you have everything you could ever need. Feelings of emptiness can serve as signals—reminding you to turn back toward Me. No matter what you are doing, I can be a co-participant with you. As you invite Me into more and more aspects of your life, you will discover a growing contentment within you. In times of adversity you can lean on Me for support; in joyous times you can celebrate with Me. I am as near as a whispered prayer—even nearer. *My banner over you is Love.*

—SARAH YOUNG
Jesus Lives

How strong is your love-bond with Jesus? What signals is your heart sending you as you ponder His perfect love? How will you respond?

March 19

There is no fear in love;
but perfect love casts out fear.
1 JOHN 4:18

The unconditional love we so desperately need if we are to become authentic comes only from God. Interestingly enough, it is when we let God love us unconditionally at a deep level that we tend to become the person He really wants us to be. It is only when we feel His total love for us that we are free to be genuine in all of our relations with others. This genuineness, I feel confident, is exactly what pleases Him most.

—NEIL CLARK WARREN
God Said It, Don't Sweat It

If God loves us unconditionally, what is keeping you from loving others in the same way?

March 20

The LORD is my light and my salvation;
Whom shall I fear?
The LORD is the strength of my life;
Of whom shall I be afraid?
PSALM 27:1

Despite God's promises, despite his infinite power and goodness and love, an element of fear seemed—and seems—reasonable to me. After all, we live in a world of people who use us and abuse
us; friends betray us and husbands leave. Furthermore, God in his
wisdom and mercy doesn't always stop the evil that makes its way to
our door. Evil has walked this earth since the Fall. From Genesis to
Revelation, there is a call from God the Father and Christ His Son: *Trust me!*
Don't be afraid!

—SHEILA WALSH
Good Morning, Lord

When have you trusted God despite your fear? In what ways did God make His
presence with you known?

March 21

But as He who called you is holy, you also be holy in all your conduct.
1 PETER 1:15

When efficient management, especially when you're good at it, trumps holy living, the lack of holiness is either not recognized or is not seen as a terribly serious problem. Compromise, including using illegitimate pleasure to relieve stress, feels warranted. People with little concern for holiness often manage their families well, they sometimes lead prospering ministries, and many are successful in their careers. But the center of God's plan has nothing to do with well-managed families, ministries, or careers. When the center of God's plan is not the center of your hope, your interior world is unstable, and your soul is weakened.

—DR. LARRY CRABB
66 Love Letters

In what ways have you made managerial efficiency a priority over personal holiness? What consequences have come from this?

_____

_____

_____

_____

_____

_____

_____

_____

_____

March 22

The fear of the LORD
is the instruction of wisdom.
PROVERBS 15:33

Freedom to choose or to reject, freedom to obey God's commands or to go contrary to them, freedom to make himself happy or miserable. For it is not the mere possession of freedom that makes life satisfying—it is what we choose to do with our freedom that determines whether or not we shall find peace with God and with ourselves.

—BILLY GRAHAM
Peace with God

What are you doing with the freedom God has given you for His glory?

March 23

The cross of our Lord Jesus Christ is
my only reason for bragging.
GALATIANS 6:14 NCV

Do you feel a need for affirmation? Does your self-esteem need attention? You don't need to drop names or show off. You need only pause at the base of the cross and be reminded of this: The maker of the stars would rather die for you than live without you. And that is a fact. So if you need to brag, brag about that.

—MAX LUCADO
Traveling Light

What changes can you make to glorify God instead of yourself?

March 24

Hope does not disappoint, because the love
of God has been poured out in our hearts by the
Holy Spirit who was given to us.
ROMANS 5:5

Have you become so overwhelmed with your own weakness and failure and sin and inability to live a life that is pleasing to God that you have begun to doubt your salvation? Then look up! Take a good, long look at the cross and remember that God remembers. He loves you, He has forgiven you, He is eternally committed to you, and you are saved! Forever! Praise God! His covenant is unconditional!

—ANNE GRAHAM LOTZ
God's Story

What steps are you taking each day to make sure your life is pleasing to God?

March 25

Greater love has no one than this, than to lay down one's life for his friends. You are my friends if you do whatever I command you.
JOHN 15:13–14

Ohne way God puts His arms around you is through your circle of friends. Whom has He brought into your life? Picture their faces. Think of the ways God has shown His love to you through them. Then, do something to show that you love them in return. Pray for them.

God's Daily Answer

Do you pray for your friends? You can support your friends in many ways. You can join them in celebrating their victories, walk beside them when they need moral support, and just share a laugh to brighten up the day. Take time now to ask God to care for them, in ways only He can. That is a true sign of friendship.

March 26

He has shown you, O man, what is good;
And what does the Lord require of you
But to do justly,
To love mercy,
And to walk humbly with your God?
MICAH 6:8

If God be everywhere present, then for a Christian to walk with God is not impossible. God is not only in heaven, but He is in earth too. Heaven is His throne, there He sits; the earth is His footstool, there He stands. He is everywhere present, therefore we may come to walk with God.

In heaven the saints rest with Him, on earth they walk with Him. To walk with God is to walk by faith. Our fellowship is with the Father. Thus we may take a turn with Him every day by faith.

There is no walk in the world so sweet as to walk with God. "They shall walk, O Lord, in the light of thy countenance" (Psalm 89:15). It is like walking among beds of spices which send forth a fragrant perfume.

—THOMAS WATSON
A Body of Divinity

What do you need to change in order to have a closer walk with God?

_____

_____

_____

_____

_____

March 27

I am with you always, even to the end of the age.
MATTHEW 28:20

It happens to every parent: your first child leaves the nest to begin her first day of school. What will the future hold? And then the day comes when you watch your last child graduate from college. Again, what will the future hold? Life is filled with fearful moments that present questions for which we have no answers. But what the future holds is really not the question. What really matters is who holds the future. In the Bible, God promises that He will never leave us nor forsake us. That promise, and a thousand others from His Word, gives us the answers to our questions about the future. The next time you find yourself wondering what the future will hold, take a minute to fill your mind with God's promises, and remember that you're not walking into the future alone.

—DAVID JEREMIAH
1 Minute a Day

Do you trust that God holds your future in his Hand? Jesus said to not worry about tomorrow, but do you find that impractical? If so, when has God ever been "practical?"

_____

_____

_____

_____

_____

_____

March 28

As the heavens are higher than the earth,
So are My ways higher than your ways,
And My thoughts than your thoughts.
ISAIAH 55:9

When we begin praying for others, we soon discover that it is easy to become discouraged at the results, which seem frustratingly slow and uneven. This is because we are entering the strange mix of divine influence and human autonomy. God never compels. . . .

His way is like the rain and the snow that gently fall to the earth, disappearing into the ground as they nourish it. When the time is right, up springs new life. No manipulation, no control; perfect freedom, perfect liberty.

—RICHARD J. FOSTER
Prayer: Finding the Heart's True Home

How can you have a better understanding of God's ways and His Word?

March 29

He leads me in the paths of righteousness
For His name's sake.
PSALM 23:3

W hat the shepherd does with the flock, our Shepherd will do with us. He will lead us to the high country. When the pasture is bare down here. God will lead us up there. He will guide us through the gate, out of the flatlands, and up the path of the mountain.

—MAX LUCADO
Traveling Light

Who do you turn to when you are facing a crisis? Is Jesus first? second? or last?

_____

_____

_____

_____

_____

_____

_____

_____

_____

_____

_____

_____

_____

March 30

The generous soul will be made rich,
And he who waters will also be watered himself.
PROVERBS 11:25

I have heard poverty in the ancient world described this way: a poor person was one who was faced at the beginning of the day with the task of finding food for that day. By that measure, most of us would be considered fabulously wealthy! Unfortunately, there are many in our world who must begin each day with the task of finding food. God wants to meet their needs, and wants to do it through those He has blessed with an abundance. The Bible is full of reasons and ways to give encouragement to those struggling to make ends meet. God is tenderhearted toward the poor and downtrodden. Look for opportunities to share with others the blessings God has bestowed on you. That is one of the best—and most rewarding—ways to please God.

—DAVID JEREMIAH
1 Minute a Day

If you don't have to struggle with finding food for yourself each day, then why not be the catalyst to fulfill God's provisionary promises in the lives of those who do struggle? In what ways can you share the blessings that God has given you with others?

March 31

I am going there to prepare a place for you.
After I go and prepare a place for you,
I will come back and take you to be with me.
JOHN 14:2–3 NCV

Note the promise of Jesus. "I will come back and take you to be with me." Jesus pledges to take us home. He does not delegate this task. He may send missionaries to teach you, angels to protect you, teachers to guide you, singers to inspire you, and physicians to heal you, but He sends no one to take you. He reserves this job for Himself.

—MAX LUCADO
Traveling Light

Name the three most important things you need to do in preparation for going to be with Jesus.

_____

_____

_____

_____

_____

_____

_____

_____

_____

_____

April

God's promises are true forever.
CHARLES STANLEY

April 1

God is love.
1 JOHN 4:8

Never question God's great love, for it is as unchangeable a part of God as is His holiness. No matter how terrible your sins, God loves you. Were it not for the love of God, none of us would ever have a chance in the future life. But God is love! And His love for us is everlasting!

—BILLY GRAHAM
Peace with God

When was the last time you went to God and thanked Him for His everlasting love?

April 2

He will teach us His ways,
And we shall walk in His paths.

MICAH 4:2

When we ask God to guide us, we have to accept by faith that He is doing so. This means that when He closes a door in our faces, we do well not to try to crash that door.

The promise is that the Shepherd will go ahead of the sheep; His method is to clear the way for us.

—CATHERINE MARSHALL
Moments that Matter

How hard is it for you to be a good student and walk in His path?

_____

_____

_____

_____

_____

_____

_____

_____

_____

_____

_____

_____

April 3

Enter into His gates with thanksgiving,
And into His courts with praise.
PSALM 100:4

Have you ever thought about what an incredible privilege it is for ordinary people, folks like you and me, to enter into the presence of Almighty God? Humbling to consider, to say the least.

Almighty God is holy . . . sinless, perfect, pure. There's absolutely no dirt hiding in the corners or under the carpet. We, on the other hand, are sinful, imperfect, and impure from carrying our sin nature in our hearts and rubbing shoulders with the world.

Yet, because God loves us and longs for relationship with us, He invites us to come to Him just as we are. We are not required to clean ourselves up or dust ourselves off. We are not obligated to attain some level of spiritual success or perfection in order to gain access to the King. We can do nothing to earn our entrance or to open the gates any wider. We can only say yes to God's invitation, accept Christ's payment by faith, and enter His gates with thanksgiving.

—KARLA DORNACHER
Give Thanks

Thank God today for the blood of Jesus, for it is only by His blood that we are able to enter into His presence.

April 4

If you have faith as a mustard seed,
you will say to this mountain, "Move from here
to there," and it will move.

MATTHEW 17:20

Don't measure the size of the mountain; talk to the One who can move it. Instead of carrying the world on your shoulders, talk to the One who holds the universe on His. Hope is a look away.

—MAX LUCADO
Traveling Light

When was the last time you asked God to move a mountain for you by faith?

_____

_____

_____

_____

_____

_____

_____

_____

_____

_____

_____

_____

April 5

Christ Jesus came into the world to save sinners.
1 TIMOTHY 1:15

God designed and created you because He loves you. . . . But you drifted in the currents of sin and were swept from Him into the world. He worked for years, making the necessary arrangements to buy you back. Finally everything was ready. The purchase price He counted out was not nickels and dimes and quarters, it was the blood of His own dear Son. As He strode victoriously out of the tomb on Easter morning, you could almost feel Him hugging you to Himself, whispering triumphantly, "You're twice mine! I made you at Creation; now I've bought you at Calvary!"

—ANNE GRAHAM LOTZ
God's Story

Have you drifted from God this past year? If so, what do you plan to do about it?

April 6

Pleasant words are like honeycomb,
Sweetness to the soul and health to the bones.
PROVERBS 16:23–24

Hugs and words of encouragement are the building blocks your children need. Their self-image and confidence is dependant on how you interact with them. Make it a habit to hug them often and acknowledge whatever they achieve in school, sports, or the arts. Your presence and open display of affection to your children will help them develop the sense of security they need. Tender, loving words will open the ears of your children, and they will eagerly look to you for wisdom and direction.

—JACK COUNTRYMAN
Time with God for Fathers

Write some encouraging words you can tell each of your children before the end of the day. Then be sure to tell them!

April 7

I am fearfully and wonderfully made;
Marvelous are Your works,
And that my soul knows very well.
PSALM 139:14

Even before Adam was created, God already had us on His mind and had determined our birthdays, our mommas and daddies, our looks, our responses to life, and even when we would die. God was thinking about us when there was only form and void in the world. And He has never stopped thinking about us.

The psalmist describes that God made every intricate part of our beings, like a master weaver who takes the finest silk threads and makes a priceless garment with precision, excellence, and exquisitely great taste. The recipient of the garment has the ability to accept this unique treasure with dignity.

Yes, that's who you are. You are a creation of God, made with His character, crafted with His DNA, and loved unconditionally by Him. God never makes junk!

—THELMA WELLS
Women of Faith Devotional Bible

How much time do you spend thanking God for the blessings He has given you? Write them down today.

April 8

The Lord is my light and my salvation;
Whom shall I fear?
The Lord is the strength of my life;
Of whom shall I be afraid?

PSALM 27:1

Webster says that "confidence" is "assurance." It comes from *con*, meaning "with," and *fideo*, meaning "faith." Confidence simply means "living with faith." It's a relationship of trust in God and yourself and others that produces inner poise under stress. If you know that Jesus is the Lord of your life, you can have the confidence that your life can be lived without limits, that your life can be a high adventure.

Faith is starting out before you know how it's going to come out. Faith does not demand miracles, but it creates an environment where miracles are the only thing that can happen. If God has given you a dream, hold to it and He will bring it to pass!

—JOHN HAGEE
Life Lessons to Live By

What does living with faith mean to you? How do you live with faith in your day-to-day life?

April 9

Your word is a lamp to my feet
And a light to my path.
PSALM 119:105

The more we know of God, the greater is our capacity to love Him. The more we love Him, the greater is our capacity to obey Him. Our new affection, however, must be made to grow. We are called to love God with our whole hearts. The new heart of flesh must be nurtured. It must be fed by the Word of God.

—R. C. SPROUL
In the Presence of God

If the Word of God is our spiritual food, how often do you come to God's table for dinner?

April 10

Take heed that you do not do your charitable deeds before men, to be seen by them. Otherwise you have no reward from your Father in heaven.
MATTHEW 6:1

Hymn writer Fanny Crosby wrote, "To God be the glory; great things He hath done!" But sometimes, because we are imperfect human beings, we seek the glory. Sometimes, when we do good deeds, we seek to glorify our achievements in a vain attempt to build ourselves up in the eyes of our neighbors. To do so is a profound mistake.

God's Word gives specific instructions about how we should approach our acts of charity: The glory must go to God, not to us. All praise belongs to the Giver of all good gifts: our Father in Heaven. We are simply conduits for His generosity, and we must remain humble . . . extremely humble.

—CRISWELL FREEMAN
Purpose for Everyday Living

Is it hard for you to be humble? When was the last time you gave God the glory for something He has done in your life?

April 11

Lead me in Your truth and teach me,
For You are the God of my salvation;
On You I wait all the day.

PSALM 25:5

Truth be known, I don't wait well. I get antsy. Hurry is my theme song. I strum my fingers on tabletops, and I don't like waiting rooms. In fact, it is a discipline for me to sit through dinner. . . . So, with this confession, you can imagine what a learning experience it has been for me to "wait all the day" on the Lord.

I want to know the Lord's ways; I want Him to teach me His paths and lead me in His truth, but I want it to happen *now*. The verse, "Be still, and know that I am God" (Psalm 46:10), was definitely written for folks wired like me. That's one thing about God's Word: it will expose weaknesses, flaws, inconsistencies, and motives for the purpose of resolve. I guess that is why the psalmist exclaims, "The entrance of Your words gives light" (Psalm 119:130).

—PATSY CLAIRMONT
Women of Faith Devotional Bible

What are you waiting on God to do in your life . . . now? Write it below and then say a prayer for peace and patience as you wait on His perfect timing.

April 12

It is He who has made us, and not we ourselves;
We are His people and the sheep of His pasture.
PSALM 100:3

Sheep aren't the only ones who need a healing touch. We also get irritated with each other, butt heads, and then get wounded. Many of our disappointments in life begin as irritations. The large portion of our problems is not lion-sized attacks, but rather the day-to-day swarm of frustrations and mishaps and heartaches.

—MAX LUCADO
Traveling Light

What are the most distracting things you have to deal with that make life difficult?

_____

_____

_____

_____

_____

_____

_____

_____

_____

_____

_____

_____

April 13

Those who know Your name will put their trust in You;
*For You, L*ORD*, have not forsaken those who seek You.*
PSALM 9:10

The tragedies most difficult to take are those that come through the failures, ignorance, carelessness, or hatred of other human beings. There are times when men seem to be working havoc with God's plans.

But God is adequate even for these situations. In order to fly, the bird must have two wings. One wing is the realization of our human helplessness; the other is the realization of God's power.

—CATHERINE MARSHALL
Moments that Matter

When trouble knocks on your door, whom do you run to first and why?

_____

_____

_____

_____

_____

_____

_____

_____

_____

_____

April 14

An inheritance quickly gained at the beginning
will not be blessed at the end.

PROVERBS 20:21 NIV

The mortality rate for humans is 100%. The fact is that someday you are going to die. People will say nice things about you, watch your casket roll out, then go back in the church and eat fried chicken and green bean casseroles. And then they are really going to talk about you!

What will they say? Will they talk about your business accomplishments and awards you have received? Will the conversation read like a résumé, listing titles you have been given and degrees earned? Or will they talk about the good things you have done for others, how well you led your family, and how you loved the Lord? Will the stories be about outrageous public actions or examples of your integrity?

—BRYANT WRIGHT
Right from the Heart

What do you think people will say about you?

April 15

*The children of men put their trust under
the shadow of Your wings.*
PSALM 36:7

When placed in the light of our awesome God, our lives find new perspective: Anxiety is replaced by hope when we see that nothing could ever be bigger than God.

Fear looses its strength when we recognize that God's power and love are a million times greater than our weakness and failure.

Peace floods our lives when we remember that all our needs are safely encompassed by God's brilliant sufficiency.

—ALICIA BRITT CHOLE
Pure Joy

What changes can be made to allow trust in the Lord to be a part of your everyday life?

_____

_____

_____

_____

_____

_____

_____

_____

_____

_____

April 16

Let the peace of God rule in your hearts, to which also
you were called in one body; and be thankful.
COLOSSIANS 3:15

S tressful days are an inevitable fact of life. And how do we best cope with the challenges of our demanding, 21st-century world? By turning our days and our lives over to God. Elisabeth Elliot writes, "If my life is surrendered to God, all is well. Let me not grab it back, as though it were in peril in His hand but would be safer in mine!"

When it comes to the inevitable challenges of this day, hand them over to God completely and without reservation. He knows your needs and will meet those needs in His own way and in His own time.

—CRISWELL FREEMAN
Purpose for Everyday Living

Write a prayer of surrender to your loving Father. Seek His strength and His power to not "grab it back"!

April 17

But now the Lord says: "Far be it from Me; for those who honor Me I will honor, and those who despise Me shall be lightly esteemed."

1 SAMUEL 2:30

Why is reverence for God's name so urgent? Because it is the mark of character. It indicates a moral and spiritual relationship to the holy God. In Washington, D.C., I once saw a man spitting on the Lincoln Memorial while a solder stood nearby saluting it. Some people spit on the sacred while others defend the sacred. The name of God is hallowed when your life is a witness to the adoration of the Lord.

—JOHN HAGEE
Life Lessons to Live By

Do your actions and words indicate reverence and adoration for the Lord?

_____

_____

_____

_____

_____

_____

_____

_____

_____

_____

_____

April 18

Anyone who is having troubles
should pray.
JAMES 5:13 NCV

Have you taken your disappointments to God? You've shared them with your neighbor, your relatives, your friends. But have you taken them to God?

Before you go anywhere else with your disappointments, go to God.

—MAX LUCADO
Traveling Light

When trouble walks in your door, does prayer become your first priority?

April 19

Teach me, O LORD, the way of Your statutes,
And I shall keep it to the end.
PSALM 119:33

As you look to the future and decide upon the direction of your life, what will you use as your roadmap? Will you trust God's Holy Word and use it as an indispensable tool to guide your steps? Or will you choose a different map to guide your steps? The map you choose will determine the quality of your journey *and* its ultimate destination.

The Bible is the ultimate guide for life; make it your guidebook as well. When you do, you can be comforted in the knowledge that your steps are guided by a Source of wisdom and truth that never fails.

—CRISWELL FREEMAN
Purpose for Everyday Living

The roadmap of life requires certain choices. What plans have you made to live for Christ each day?

_____

_____

_____

_____

_____

_____

_____

_____

_____

April 20

*For this purpose I have raised you up, that I may show My power
in you, and that My name may be declared in all the earth.*
EXODUS 9:16

A friend of mine read the entire Bible when she was twelve. When she finished, she said to her mother, "Wow! God is really, really God." What a statement! My little friend understood that God is powerful and accomplishes His purposes even when it makes no sense to us. He is strong and good, whether we recognize it or not.

And He is God. He's not afraid of being misunderstood by anyone. He always does what is right, in order to fulfill His purpose. The strength of that and His absolute sovereignty give me security. He is really, really God.

—MARY GRAHAM
Women of Faith Devotional Bible

Do you trust that God really is God and can handle any situation? Do you trust that He always does what is right in order to fulfill His purpose?

April 21

The steps of a good man are ordered by the Lord,
And He delights in his way.
Though he fall, he shall not be utterly cast down;
For the Lord upholds him with His hand.
PSALM 37:23–24

God has promised that when we walk faithfully with Him and when He becomes an integral part of our everyday lives, His spirit will guide us in such a way that His protection will surround everything we say and do. Though we would like to be perfect, the truth is that we make mistakes, we fall down, and we become a disappointment to ourselves and those we love. God wants to take us gently by the hand and lead us, so that we are blessed and He is glorified.

—JACK COUNTRYMAN
Time with God for Mothers

It is easy to be hard on ourselves when we have made a mistake. But do you move on from that mistake and continue to walk in God's love and forgiveness, or do you continue to wallow in your own pity, not allowing yourself to be forgiven, and therefore nullify God's glory?

April 22

You anoint my head with oil;
My cup runs over.
PSALM 23:5

We were created for relationship . . . with God and with others. Our lives are filled with a variety of people whom God uses to fill our cups and bless our lives. Some we know well; some we barely know at all. We have family, friends, and neighbors. We have pastors, doctors, and dentists. We depend on bank tellers, mail carriers, and grocery store clerks. We labor together with our co-workers on the job and in ministry. And of course we can't forget teachers, coaches, and other parents who play such a big part in the growth of our children.

But remember . . . not even the people we love and those who love us can ever fill our deepest relational needs. Our cups can only overflow when Jesus is our very Best Friend of all. He knows us better than anyone else, and He loves us more than anyone else loves us. He gave His life for us, and He alone is the perfect Friend.

—KARLA DORNACHER
Give Thanks

Do you sometimes depend on your relationship with family and friends, or even your spouse, but forget that you ultimately need to depend on God to meet your deepest relational needs?

April 23

*Give all your worries to
him, because he cares about you.*
1 PETER 5:7 NCV

Maybe you don't want to trouble God with your hurts. After all, *He's got famines and pestilence and wars; He won't care about my little struggles,* you think. Why don't you let Him decide that? He cared enough about a wedding to provide the wine. He cared enough about Peter's tax payment to give him a coin. He cared enough about the woman at the well to give her answers.

—MAX LUCADO
Traveling Light

What worries do you need to give God today?

_____

_____

_____

_____

_____

_____

_____

_____

_____

_____

_____

April 24

But if the Spirit of Him who raised Jesus from the dead dwells in you,
He who raised Christ from the dead will also give life to your
mortal bodies through His Spirit who dwells in you.
ROMANS 8:11

Here's a piece of American constitutional trivia you may not know. The eighteenth amendment to the United States Constitution banned alcohol as a beverage in America in 1920, but the twenty-first amendment repealed the eighteenth amendment thirteen years later. In other words, the legalized prohibition of alcohol failed. That grand experiment in legislating morality proved that alcohol is not the primary problem. Nor are guns, sex, or gambling. The problem is a lack of self-control. And the Bible says self-control can't be legislated either. Fortunately for us, God offers to live in us and control our desires with the power of His indwelling presence for our good and for the good of those around us. When we surrender to His transforming Spirit, we give ourselves the opportunity to become more like Christ.

—DAVID JEREMIAH
1 Minute a Day

How amazing is the truth and promise of God that His Spirit, His transforming
Spirit, lives in us! Does that give you hope that you will be able to have the power and
discipline to live a fruitful and godly life?

April 25

I will put my Spirit within you.
EZEKIEL 36:27

Let us pray to God, that as He is a Spirit, so He will give us of His Spirit. The essence of God is incommunicable, but not the motions—the presence and influences of His Spirit. When the sun shines in a room, not the body of the sun is there, but the light, heat, and influence of the sun. God has made a promise of His Spirit.

Turn promises into prayers. "O Lord, thou who art a Spirit, give me of Thy Spirit . . . thy enlightening, sanctifying, quickening Spirit." We cannot do any duty without it.

—THOMAS WATSON
A Body of Divinity

What are some ways the Holy Spirit has lead you and influenced you when you needed it most?

_____

_____

_____

_____

_____

_____

_____

_____

_____

_____

April 26

I am the good shepherd.
The good shepherd gives His life for the sheep.
JOHN 10:11

Real meaning for your life is found in the glorious dawn of God's story, which breaks into full revelation in the Person of Jesus Christ.
Because He emptied Himself of all but love, you can be filled.
Because His body was broken, your life can be whole.
Because His blood was shed, your sin can be forgiven.
Because He finished His Father's work, your life has worth.

—ANNE GRAHAM LOTZ
God's Story

What does it mean to you that Jesus the Good Shepherd gave His life for you?

April 27

When you pass through the waters, I will be with you;
And through the rivers, they shall not overflow you.
ISAIAH 43:2

G od does not whisk us at once to Glory. We go on living in a fractured
world, suffering in one way or another the effects of sin—sometimes
our own, sometimes others'. Yet I have come to understand even suffering,
through the transforming power of the Cross, as a gift, for in this broken
world, in our sorrow, He gives us Himself. In our loneliness He comes to
meet us.

—ELISABETH ELLIOT
Keep a Quiet Heart

When were some times God's protection has delivered you from trouble?

_____

_____

_____

_____

_____

_____

_____

_____

_____

_____

_____

April 28

The sacrifices of God are a broken spirit,
A broken and a contrite heart—
These, O God, You will not despise.

PSALM 51:17

Jesus told the parable of the Prodigal Son to dramatize what He meant by the word *repent*. When the Prodigal Son repented he didn't just sit still and feel sorry about all his sins. He wasn't passive and limp about it. He didn't stay where he was, surrounded by the swine. He got up and left! He turned his feet in the other direction. He sought out his father and humbled himself before him, and then he was forgiven.

—BILLY GRAHAM
Peace with God

From this verse, what makes the difference in the Father's attitude and action toward His children?

April 29

If any of you lacks wisdom,
let him ask of God, who gives to all liberally . . .
and it will be given to him.
JAMES 1:5

God is not only wise, He is the ground of wisdom. He is not only beautiful, He is the source and standard of all beauty. He is not merely good, He is the norm of all goodness.

He is the source, the ground, the norm, the fountainhead of all love.

—R. C. SPROUL
Loved by God

What have you learned from your times of testing and difficulties that will give you a new prespective on trials in your life?

_____

_____

_____

_____

_____

_____

_____

_____

_____

_____

_____

April 30

The throne of God and of the Lamb shall be in it,
and His servants shall serve Him.

REVELATION 22:3

Many people ask, "Well, what will we do in heaven? Just sit down and enjoy the luxuries of life?" No. The Bible indicates that we will serve God. There will be work to do for God. Our very beings will praise God. It will be a time of total joy, service, laughter, singing, and praise to God. Imagine serving Him forever and never growing tired!

—BILLY GRAHAM
Peace with God

When you think about heaven, what picture comes to your mind?

May

Because God's promises are always true,
you can have hope!
ANNE GRAHAM LOTZ

May 1

I will not forget you.
See, I have inscribed you on the palms of My hands.
ISAIAH 49:15–16

Did you think God's silence in your life meant He had forgotten you? Oh, no! God says He has engraved your name on the palms of His hands. He says that a mother could forget her nursing baby at mealtime before He could forget you! You are in God's heart and on His mind every moment. He is fully informed of your circumstances and will bring about change when He knows the time is right.

—ANNE GRAHAM LOTZ
God's Story

When you hear someone say "God has forgotten me," how do you respond?

_____

_____

_____

_____

_____

_____

_____

_____

_____

_____

_____

_____

May 2

God has given us eternal life, and this life is in his Son.
He who has the Son has life; he who does not
have the Son of God does not have life.
1 JOHN 5:11–12 NIV

Eternal life isn't just living forever in heaven with God—although that's certainly part of it. Your promise for eternal life includes the here and now. If you've entrusted yourself to God's care and received His gift of salvation, you have the reality of eternal life today. You don't have to wait to die an earthly death before you can enjoy it.

The Bible says that God's goodness and mercy will follow you all the days of your life. So why live another day without hope, without joy, without meaning. Reach out to God. Trade in your old life for a new one, and start living life to the fullest—all the days of your life here on Earth—and later in heaven.

God's Daily Answer

How would realizing that your eternal life with God has (if you have accepted it) already begun, change your perception on life?

May 3

*God will always give what is right to his people . . .
and he will not be slow to answer them.*
LUKE 18:7 NCV

When we come to God, we make requests; we don't make demands. We come with high hopes and a humble heart. We state what we want, but we pray for what is right. And if God gives us the prison of Rome instead of the mission of Spain, we accept it because we know "God will always give what is right to his people." We go to him. We bow before him, and we trust in him.

—MAX LUCADO
Traveling Light

What requests have you made to God that He has been slow to answer?

May 4

*May [He] establish your hearts
blameless in holiness before our God.*
1 THESSALONIANS 3:13

No matter how soiled your past, no matter how snarled your present, no matter how hopeless your future seems to be—there is a way out. There is a sure, safe, everlasting way out—but there is only one! You have only one choice to make.

You can go on being miserable, discontented, frightened, and unhappy. Or you can decide now to become the person Jesus promised you could be.

—BILLY GRAHAM
Peace with God

What changes do you need to make to be "blameless in holiness" before God?

_____

_____

_____

_____

_____

_____

_____

_____

_____

_____

_____

May 5

The fruit of the Spirit is in all goodness, righteousness, and truth.
EPHESIANS 5:9

Then Jesus left the earth, He gave us the Comforter, the Counselor, the very presence of God. When the Holy Spirit fills you, it is as if Jesus Himself takes the helm of your life and navigates your course. When you elect the guidance system called the Holy Spirit, your life moves in the right direction. You are filled with the powerful sense of being deeply loved, since everything about Jesus' teaching focuses on love. You know you have enormous worth as a human being.

—NEIL CLARK WARREN
God Said It, Don't Sweat It

What steps have you made to reflect your walk with Christ?

May 6

I waited patiently for the Lord;
And He inclined to me,
And heard my cry.
He also brought me up out of a horrible pit, . . .
And set my feet upon a rock, . . .
He has put a new song in my mouth—
Praise to our God.

PSALM 40:1–3

God knows your heart. He knows which mess-ups you're concerned about. He knows that you wonder if he still hears you when you pray or cares about you when you stumble. He also knows the shame that arises when you consider facing what you have done and start walking the long path home. But hear this truth: with God, all things can be made new. Your past is just that, but your future in him is limitless. All God looks for is your desire to begin moving in the right direction, and he will be there—and not just passively, but anxiously waiting to embrace you. You are loved; you are loved; you are loved!

—SHEILA WALSH
Good Morning, Lord

What specific message of reassurance would you like to hear from the Lord? Sit quietly with Him, share your heart, and listen for His voice of love.

May 7

*In the beginning was the Word, and
the Word was with God, and the Word was God.
He was in the beginning with God.*

JOHN 1:1–2

Jesus is the living expression of what is on God's mind. But He is more. He is the living expression of what is on God's heart. But He is even more. He is the very heart of the Almighty God of the universe laid bare for all to see!

Do you want to know what is on the mind of God? Then look at Jesus! Do you want to know the will of God? Then look at Jesus! Do you want to know what is in the heart of God? Then look at Jesus!

—ANNE GRAHAM LOTZ
Just Give Me Jesus

If someone were to ask you to describe Jesus and the life He lived, what would you say?

_____

_____

_____

_____

_____

_____

_____

_____

_____

_____

_____

May 8

He has made His wonderful works to be remembered;
The LORD is gracious and full of compassion.

PSALM 111:4

God always does what is right because . . . that is all He is able to do. He can only do what is right because in His being He is altogether righteous. Because God is love, He is loving in His nature, and all of His actions reflect that love.

—R. C. SPROUL
Loved by God

When was the last time you gave thanks to God for His grace and compassion?

May 9

If we are faithless, He remains faithful;
He cannot deny Himself.
2 TIMOTHY 2:13

Our moods may shift, but God's doesn't. Our minds may change, but God's doesn't.

Our devotion may falter, but God's never does. Even if we are faithless, He is faithful, for He cannot betray himself. He is a sure God.

—MAX LUCADO
Traveling Light

When was a time your faith was tested? What did you do?

May 10

Yet I am always with you; you hold me by my right hand.
You guide me with your counsel, and afterward you will take me into glory.
PSALM 73:23–24 NIV

I offer you inexpressible and glorious Joy—straight from heaven itself. This *triumphant, heavenly Joy* can be found only in Me. It is easy for you to slide, ever so gradually, from exulting in Me to living for the next spiritual "high." Though I do grant you some heavenly pleasure while you still live on earth, this is mainly to whet your appetite for the next life. Do not underestimate the brokenness of the world where you live now. Your exuberant enjoyment of My Presence will always intermingle with the sorrows of living in this fallen world—until *I take you into Glory*.

Someday you will see Me face to Face, but for now *you love Me without having seen Me. You believe in Me even though you do not see Me.* This is a most blessed way to live, and it demonstrates your membership in My royal family. Your love for Me—My unseen Person—is not irrational or whimsical. It is a response to My boundless Love for you—dramatically displayed on the cross and verified by My resurrection. You worship a risen, living Savior! *Blessed are those who have not seen Me and yet have believed.*

—SARAH YOUNG
Jesus Lives

What difference does an eternal perspective make as you live your life here on earth today?

May 11

*It is God . . . who has shown in our hearts to
give the light of the knowledge of the glory of God.*
2 CORINTHIANS 4:6

We do not understand many mysteries, but we accept by faith the fact that at the moment we repent of sin and turn by faith to Jesus Christ we are born again.

It is the infusion of divine life into the human soul, . . . whereby we become the children of God. We receive the breath of God. Christ through the Holy Spirit takes up residence in our hearts. We are attached to God for eternity.

—BILLY GRAHAM
Peace with God

At what age did you accept Christ? Write down your relationship with God today.

_____

_____

_____

_____

_____

_____

_____

_____

_____

_____

May 12

*We all show the Lord's glory, and we are being changed to be
like him. This change in us brings ever greater glory,
which comes from the Lord, who is the Spirit.*
2 CORINTHIANS 3:18 NCV

I must tell you that I grew up a very selfish, proud, and materialist individual. But when, at the age of nineteen, I got saved, the first thing I wanted to do was give. I wanted to give to everyone I could. I wanted to bless others and help them know what I had found.

One of the greatest blessings I've experienced through giving is being able to see God's kingdom enlarge, to see ministries advance, to see churches grow, and to see broken people become whole—all because of obedience in giving.

One thing I want you to understand . . . I was lost and without hope. I didn't know Christ. Jesus gave His all to save an arrogant, prideful nobody. So I can do no less than give my all for Him.

—ROBERT MORRIS
The Blessed Life

Would you give tithes and offerings even if your only reward was salvation through Christ Jesus? Will you commit this day to live the life of a giver regardless of the rewards?

May 13

Jesus Christ is the same yesterday, today, and forever.
HEBREWS 13:8

That simple, straightforward statement holds great riches to be uncovered. Consider the qualities of God that mean so much to us as believers: His presence with us, His faithfulness, and His goodness. What about His holiness, justice, and perfection? Think of His redemptive power and His ability to bring beauty out of ashes. And the fact that He is all-powerful, all-knowing, and sovereign over the unfolding history of this world.

Whatever divine characteristics we think of, we can know that God has always been that way and will always remain that way. Find comfort and peace in that assurance.

—HENRY AND RICHARD BLACKABY
Discovering God's Daily Agenda

List the qualities of God that are especially meaningful to you during this season of your life.

May 14

He who has My commandments and keeps them, it is he who loves Me.
JOHN 14:21

If I could simplify the Christian life to one thing, it would be obedience. I don't mean just external obedience but a spirit of obedience.

One evidence of spiritual maturity is loving God enough to obey Him even when it is difficult. God is glorified most when we willingly obey Him no matter what the cost. Each time we obey, we grow spiritually, and each time we disobey, we retard our growth.

—JOHN MACARTHUR
Truth for Today

When was a difficult time or circumstance when you were obedient (even though it was hard) and did what you knew God wanted you to do? How did the Lord bless you in the end?

May 15

Jesus looked at them and said, "With man this is impossible,
but with God all things are possible."
MATTHEW 19:26 NIV

With Me all things are possible. When you bump into massive difficulties on your life-path, I want you to *consider it pure Joy*. As you bounce off these "impossibilities," *My everlasting arms* are wide open—ready to catch you, calm you, and help you do what does not seem possible. You can be joyful in the midst of perplexing problems because I am *God your Savior*. I have already accomplished the greatest miracle—saving you from your sins. If you keep looking to Me, your resurrected Lord and King, your pessimism will eventually yield to courage. Though you are an earthbound creature in many ways, your soul shares in My eternal victory.

Since I am infinite, "impossibilities" are My specialty. I delight in them because they display My Glory so vividly. They also help you live the way I intended: in joyful, trusting dependence on Me. The next time you face an "impossible" situation, turn to Me immediately with a hopeful heart. Acknowledge your total inadequacy, and cling to Me—relying on My infinite sufficiency. *All things are possible with Me!*

—SARAH YOUNG
Jesus Lives

Recall a time when you saw God do something that is humanly impossible. How can that memory build up your faith today?

May 16

Call to Me, and I will answer you,
and show you great and mighty things,
which you do not know.
JEREMIAH 33:3

Swings give a feeling of weightlessness—for a few moments you bypass the laws of gravity. For a few moments you fly!

Dreams do much the same thing. Dreams crash the confines of what is and what has been. As our minds dare to see the unseen, our imagination fuels our faith and we begin to trust God for something more.

Some folks are afraid to dream. But connected to God, it is safe to dream. There is freedom to let faith take wings.

—ALICIA BRITT CHOLE
Pure Joy

God has swung the door wide open for you to come to Him in prayer. What do you need to call to Him about today?

May 17

Surely goodness and mercy shall follow me
All the days of my life;
And I will dwell in the house of the LORD
Forever.
PSALM 23:6

What a huge statement. Look at the size of it! Goodness and mercy follow the child of God each and every day! Think of the days that lie ahead. What do you see? Days at home with only toddlers? God will be at your side. Days in a dead-end job? He will walk you through. Days of loneliness? He will take your hand. Surely goodness and mercy shall follow me—not some, not most, not nearly all—but all the days of my life.

—MAX LUCADO
Traveling Light

God promises us goodness and mercy when we are one with Him. Where are you in your oneness with God?

_____

_____

_____

_____

_____

_____

_____

_____

_____

May 18

Put on the whole armor of God, that you may be
able to stand against the wiles of the devil.
EPHESIANS 6:11

E ven when God allows us to experience a season of testing, he doesn't leave us alone or unarmed . . . he has provided us with the armor of God. When we are wearing the belt of God's truth, we recognize Satan's lies. When we have the breastplate of righteousness in place, we are confident of our standing as forgiven and beloved. When we hold up the shield of faith, we "will be able to quench all the fiery darts of the wicked one" (Ephesians 6:16). The helmet of salvation protects our mind from the enemy's lies, God's Word is our sword of protection against deceit and confusion, and, shod with the gospel of peace, we can move forward in confidence and strength.

—SHEILA WALSH
Good Morning, Lord

When have you been most aware of the very real power of Satan in your life? What did you learn from that experience?

May 19

It is good that a man should both hope and quietly wait
for the salvation of the Lord.
LAMENTATIONS 3:26 KJV

It isn't easy to focus on what you cannot see. Take parenthood, for instance. Parents have to focus on the future as they raise their children, instilling qualities that will help their children reach their potential. You don't see the results of your work until your kids are much further down the road. But, hope is what keeps you committed to the journey even when things don't look very promising.

Where is hope leading you today? Hope is the fuel that keeps you going, when what you're hoping for is still somewhere down the road. God knows what that is. He's always there to help you refuel. When your tank is low, turn to Him.

God's Daily Answer

When things get tough, do you tend to tell yourself that God will work things out, or do you actually turn to Him and lay your burdens down on Him?

May 20

You will seek the LORD your God,
and you will find Him if you seek Him with
all your heart and with all your soul.
DEUTERONOMY 4:29

Do you know God?

If Adam knew Him as a beloved Father, if Abraham knew Him as a Friend, if Moses knew Him as a Redeemer, if David knew Him as his Shepherd, if Daniel knew Him as the Lion Tamer, if Mary Magdalene knew Him as the Bondage Breaker, if Martha knew Him as the Promise Keeper, surely you and I can know Him too!

—ANNE GRAHAM LOTZ
Just Give Me Jesus

How well do you know God? What is the importance of spending time with Him?

_____

_____

_____

_____

_____

_____

_____

_____

_____

_____

_____

_____

May 21

You are God,
Ready to pardon,
Gracious and merciful,
Slow to anger,
Abundant in kindness.
NEHEMIAH 9:17

Do you feel like God could never forgive you for the things you have done in your life? Be assured there is nothing you could do that God cannot forgive. He sees and knows every one of your thoughts and words and deeds. He saw them before you were born.

That's why He sent His Son Jesus to carry all your sins and misdeeds to the cross, where they would be atoned for once and for all. The payment for your debt was so great that it covers the very worst that human nature can conceive.

Today, receive God's loving forgiveness for your sins and missteps. Let Him wash you white as snow on the inside. Then go and be a better person for Him.

God's Daily Answer

Have you received God's gift of forgiveness for your sins? How have you become a better person for doing so?

_____

_____

_____

_____

_____

May 22

*And ye became followers of us, and of the Lord, having received
the word in much affliction, with joy of the Holy Ghost.*
1 THESSALONIANS 1:6 KJV

We glorify God by walking cheerfully. It brings glory to God when the
world sees a Christian has that within him that can make him cheerful in the worst times; that can enable him, with the nightingale, to sing
with a thorn at this breast. The people of God have ground for cheerfulness. They are justified and adopted, and this creates inward peace; it makes
music within, whatever storms are without. If we consider what Christ has
wrought for us by his blood, and wrought in us by his Spirit, it is a ground
of great cheerfulness, and this cheerfulness glorifies God.

—THOMAS WATSON
A Body of Divinity

What is one thing you can do to glorify God today?

_____

_____

_____

_____

_____

_____

_____

_____

_____

May 23

I have seen his ways, and will heal him;
I will also lead him,
And restore comforts to him
And to his mourners.
ISAIAH 57:18

A few generations ago, if something broke, it was fixed. Today, we live in a throw-away world where things are designed to be replaced when they break. That's okay for toasters and hair dryers, but it doesn't work too well with the human heart. When your heart breaks, you can't go to the big-box discount store and get a new one. Fortunately, broken hearts can be put together again—but it takes God to do it, the Bible says. He's the only One with the power to restore us when we've been hurt. If your heart is broken, don't discard it. Let God take a look. It may take a little time and trust, but rest assured that He's never seen one yet He couldn't mend.

—DAVID JEREMIAH
1 Minute a Day

Do you find it hard to trust others because your heart has been broken so many times?

May 24

Who shall bring a charge against God's elect?
It is God who justifies.
ROMANS 8:33

Your sins have been forgiven. God has buried them in the depths of the sea and placed them behind His back of forgetfulness. Every sin is completely wiped out. You stood before God as a debtor, you received your discharge, you have become reconciled to God. You are now a child of God.

—BILLY GRAHAM
Peace with God

If God the Supreme Judge justifies, then who is going to successfully bring a charge against us?

May 25

He who sacrifices thank offerings honors me,
and he prepares the way
so that I may show him the salvation of God.
PSALM 50:23 NIV

L et's be honest. During certain seasons of our lives, our circumstances are such that we can be hard-pressed to find anything to be thankful for. When you lose your job. When you lose someone you love. When you lose your health. When you lose a dream . . . security . . . hope. Life here on earth is full of losses that can leave you tongue-tied when it comes to giving thanks.

But in those moments, more than in any others, thanksgiving will be your strength as you praise God for who He is, as you place your confidence in His provision and His promises for your life.

According to Psalm 50:23, in our times of trouble, thanksgiving that rises despite our circumstances and emotions is not impossible. It is, however, a choice. It is a decision we make in obedience to God's Word and according to His will for our lives, and it is a decision that honors God and moves His heart. Somehow, when we offer up these bittersweet sacrifices to God, a door in the heavenly realms opens, and our thanksgiving prepares the way for God to reveal Himself to us in a new and powerful way.

—KARLA DORNACHER
Give Thanks

Your sacrifices of thanksgiving open a door for God to move on your behalf. Does this
encourage your heart and give you hope?

_____

_____

May 26

All things were made through Him, and
without Him nothing was made that was made.
JOHN 1:3

God created atoms and angels and ants, crocodiles and chiggers and clouds, diamonds and dust and dinosaurs, raindrops and sweat drops, dewdrops and blood drops, and me! And you!

The greatness of His power to create and design and form and mold and make and build and arrange defies the limits of our imagination. And since He created everything, there is nothing beyond His power to fix or mend or heal or restore.

—ANNE GRAHAM LOTZ
Just Give Me Jesus

Since God created everything and is all-powerful, what does He need to heal or
restore in your life?

May 27

The just shall live by faith.
ROMANS 1:17

Faith actually means surrender and commitment to the claims of Christ. It means an acknowledgment of sin and a turning to Christ. We do not know Christ through the five physical senses, but we know Him through the sixth sense that God has given every person—that ability to believe.

—BILLY GRAHAM
Peace with God

In your own words, what does it mean to live by faith?

_____

_____

_____

_____

_____

_____

_____

_____

_____

_____

_____

_____

_____

_____

_____

May 28

Confess your trespasses to one another, and pray for one another, that you may be healed. The effective, fervent prayer of a righteous man avails much.
JAMES 5:16

Someone has said that prayer is like the breath of life: you cannot exist spiritually without it. Prayer is also a great connector in our relationship with other Christian brothers and sisters. God has designed this world in such a way that so many of our needs are met only through mutual interdependence on fellow believers, and our singular dependence on God. When a father comes to God in earnest prayer, . . . his life will be changed and God will be glorified.

—JACK COUNTRYMAN
Time with God for Fathers

Do you have a brother or sister in Christ whom you can pray with and for? If not, commit to asking God to cross your path with someone whom you can.

May 29

I will take you as My people, and I will be your God.
EXODUS 6:7

As a child with seven older siblings, we only had bare essentials in our tiny house. My cousins, though, had everything . . . beds, rooms, TV, candy on demand, and space. Something about their house gave me a longing. On more than one occasion, I begged to spend the night with them. Inevitably I couldn't make it through the night. My uncle would have to take me home. "I can't stay here," I would cry, "I need people who belong to me." So home I went to crawl into a bed full of sisters.

There's nothing quite like having your own people. People who know and understand you, care about what concerns you, understand your idiosyncrasies. It's much better than "stuff." But that's nothing compared to having our own God. Belonging to Him is liberating. It sets us free and satisfies our longings.

—MARY GRAHAM
Women of Faith Devotional Bible

Is there any "stuff" you are trying to draw satisfaction from rather than our gracious God?

May 30

I will never leave you nor forsake you.
HEBREWS 13:5

The Love that calls us into being, woos us to Himself, makes us His bride, lays down His life for us, and daily crowns us with loving-kindness and tender mercy, will not, no matter how it may appear in our loneliness, abandon us. "I will never [the Greek has five different negatives here], never, never, never, never leave you or forsake you."

—ELISABETH ELLIOT
Keep a Quiet Heart

List some of the blessings you receive from accepting this message.

May 31

But he who endures to the end shall be saved.
MATTHEW 24:13

How do you overcome those moments in life when you feel inferior, when you feel intimidated or inadequate in the face of a crisis? When Satan comes at you like a roaring lion, trying to overwhelm you with fear and uncertainty, what do you do? The first thing you need to do is give up every thought about quitting. Never surrender to fear or let worry master you. Never play the victim role. You're never going to stand in the winner's circle if you don't finish the race. Quitters never win, and winners never quit. In Jesus' name, you are more than a conqueror, and the victory is yours.

—JOHN HAGEE
Life Lessons to Live By

Do you have a problem with becoming overwhelmed and buckling under pressure? If we are more than conquerors in Jesus' name, what do you think you should do in these types of situations?

June

*Trusting God is doing the
greatest thing anybody can do.*
ELISABETH ELLIOT

June 1

Truly my soul quietly waits for God;
From Him comes my salvation.
PSALM 62:1

The world seems to grow louder day by day, and our senses seem to be invaded at every turn. Our task, as believers, is to carve out moments of silence in a world filled with noise.

If we are to maintain righteous minds and compassionate hearts, we must take time each day for prayer and for meditation. We must make ourselves still in the presence of our Creator. We must quiet our minds and our hearts so that we might sense God's will and His love.

—CRISWELL FREEMAN
Purpose for Everyday Living

How would you reorder your life's priorities in order to have more time to be still and experience quiet, peaceful moments with God?

June 2

*Let us consider one another in order to stir up love and
good works, not forsaking the assembling of ourselves together,
as is the manner of some, but exhorting one another.*

HEBREWS 10:24–25

I love what Billy Graham says: "Being in church no more makes you a Christian than being in a garage makes you a car." No, you do not have to go to church to be a Christian, but attending church serves a three-fold purpose to help us to grow in our faith.

1. To worship with other believers.
2. Church is a place of Christian fellowship, and Lone Ranger-Christians don't do well in the journey of faith.
3. Church is a place where we can use our gifts in service and ministry.

While you don't have to come to church to be a Christian, failure to attend retards your spiritual growth. And when you're not in church, you miss out on the rich fellowship of other meaningful relationships with believers.

—BRYANT WRIGHT
Right from the Heart

What about you? Is attending, serving, and sharing your gifts in church a priority in your life?

June 3

*His divine power has given to us all things
that pertain to life and godliness,
through the knowledge of Him who called us
by glory and virtue.*

2 PETER 1:3

God is bigger than we think and greater than we think. Nothing is beyond His ability, whether it's a problem to solve, a marriage to reconcile, a memory to heal, a guilty conscience to cleanse, or a sin to forgive.

If God has the power to create and sustain the universe, how can you think His power is insufficient for you? He is more than able to sustain your marriage and your ministry, your faith and your finances, your hope and your health.

—ANNE GRAHAM LOTZ
Just Give Me Jesus

Thank Jesus for giving you His divine power to live for Him in a lost world.

June 4

*For the L*ORD *gives wisdom.*
PROVERBS 2:6

Ibelieve God will provide the wisdom to understand any trial if we will ask Him. If we don't ask, the Lord may allow the trial to continue until we demonstrate that we have learned to be dependent on Him through the trial.

If you lack wisdom, you're commanded to ask God for it. Wisdom is never withheld from a believer who needs it and asks for it as he perseveres through a trial. Isn't that a wonderful promise? Sometimes we don't ask; we do everything *but* ask God. We ought to be on our knees crying out from our hearts for God to give us His direction.

—JOHN MACARTHUR
Truth for Today

What is a situation in which you need God's wisdom? Open your heart now and ask Him for understanding and perseverance.

June 5

Neither death nor life, nor angels
nor principalities nor powers, nor things present
nor things to come, nor height nor depth,
nor any other created thing, shall
be able to separate us from the love of God.
ROMANS 8:38–39

In this passage the apostle sets forth the principle that gripped the reformers of the sixteenth century: *Deus pro nobis*, which means simply "God for us." The source of Christian comfort is that God is for us and is on our side. To know that God is for us is to know that no one and nothing can ever prevail against us.

—R. C. SPROUL
Loved by God

If God is for us and no created thing can separate us, why do we struggle with our own security?

June 6

Draw near to God and
He will draw near to you.
JAMES 4:8

Some people find it easier to draw closer to God in magnificent buildings and with some form of ritual. Others find they can seek God only in stark simplicity. Some people find themselves more comfortable with formality, others feel more at home with informality.

The important thing is not *how* we do it, but the sincerity and depth of purpose *with which* we do it.

—BILLY GRAHAM
Peace with God

Why do we sometimes doubt our relationship with God?

June 7

The LORD is good to all; he has compassion on all he has made.
PSALM 145:9 NIV

Imagine what it would be like to see the world through God's eyes. How would you feel about the woman in the wheelchair at the grocery store? The neighbor kid who's just found out his folks are getting a divorce? The homeless guy on the park bench?

Seeing individuals the way God does makes you want to put love into action and help. That's compassion kicking in. Compassion doesn't just feel sorry for people. It strives to make a positive difference in their lives. So, ask God to help you see through His eyes—then let you know how you can help. Even if the only action you can take is to pray, your compassion can make a difference in the world.

God's Daily Answer

List some people you can think of right now that you know need love and compassion in their lives. How can you help them?

_____

_____

_____

_____

_____

_____

_____

_____

June 8

Is anyone among you suffering?
Let him pray . . . and the Lord will raise him up.
JAMES 5:13, 15

Depression is a gloomy mindset that from time to time smudges our moods. At one time or another it afflicts us all. The waves of depression crash upon the shores of our lives in ever-increasing surges. But is it hopeless? No. Christ is always the key to winning over our dour moods. The issue of our wholeness lies in making Christ the Lord over all circumstances.

—CALVIN MILLER
Into the Depths of God

What area of your life do you choose not to include in prayer?

June 9

Even to your old age, I am He,
And even to gray hairs I will carry you!
I have made, and I will bear;
Even I will carry, and will deliver you.
ISAIAH 46:4

Old age sure ain't for sissies. In Ecclesiastes, King Solomon would agree. He wrote of how the things we take for granted when we're young cause us to lose delight in living when we're old.

Our eyesight grows dim—we start with reading glasses and then move to bifocals. Our hearing grows weak. We're constantly saying "huh?" to our spouse. We have time to sleep late but we wake up early. Our hands start to tremble. Our desire for sex diminishes.

Old age isn't for sissies, and without God it can be meaningless. But with God, there is wisdom, strength, joy, and the hope that when the body finally gives out, there is life—real life—in heaven with God. It's something to remember when you're young and when you're old.

—BRYANT WRIGHT
Right from the Heart

Whether you're young or old, what are the challenges you face to live life to the fullest for God?

June 10

When Your words came, I ate them;
they were my joy and my heart's delight,
for I bear Your name,
LORD God Almighty.
JEREMIAH 15:16 NIV

For me, good company enriches any meal. And Jeremiah felt the same way. His favorite food was God's Word in the company of . . . God Himself!

What an incredible banquet God gives us through His Word. The Scriptures, when ingested, bring delight to our hearts and energy to our spirits. God's Word is thoroughly nutritious and always fresh.

—ALICIA BRITT CHOLE
Pure Joy

What kind of appetite do you have for God's Word?

June 11

Whoever desires to save his life will lose it,
but whoever loses his life for My sake will find it.
MATTHEW 16:25

I believe the secret of happiness lies imbedded in those words, painful though they appear to be. I have observed that when any of us embarks on the pursuit of happiness for ourselves, it eludes us. Often I've asked myself why. It must be because happiness comes to us only as a dividend. When we become absorbed in something demanding and worthwhile above and beyond ourselves, happiness seems to be there as a by-product of self-giving.

—CATHERINE MARSHALL
Moments that Matter

What is your greatest desire?

_____

_____

_____

_____

_____

_____

_____

_____

_____

_____

_____

_____

June 12

The number of His years
is unsearchable.
JOB 36:26 NASB

We may search out the moment the first wave slapped on a shore or the first star burst in the sky, but we'll never find the first moment when God was God, for there is no moment when God was not God. He has never not been, for He is eternal. God is not bound by time.

—MAX LUCADO
He Chose the Nails

What comes to mind when you think about the beginning of time as it relates to God?

June 13

And he said:
"The LORD is my rock and my fortress and my deliverer;
The God of my strength, in whom I will trust."
2 SAMUEL 22:2–3

Do the demands of this day threaten to overwhelm you? If so, you must rely not upon your own resources, but also upon the promises of your Father in heaven. God will hold your hand and walk with you every day of your life if you let Him. Even if your circumstances are difficult, trust the Father. His love is eternal and His goodness endures forever.

—CRISWELL FREEMAN
Purpose for Everyday Living

What demands threaten to overwhelm you today? Write them below and lay them at the feet of God's throne. Trust Him to be with you every step of your way.

_____

_____

_____

_____

_____

_____

_____

_____

_____

_____

_____

June 14

You shall not take the name of the LORD your God in vain, for the
LORD will not hold him guiltless who takes His name in vain.
EXODUS 20:7

General George Washington posted this notice for all his officers to read to every enlisted man in the army: "The general is sorry to inform that the foolish, wicked practice of cursing, a vice heretofore little known in the American army, is growing in fashion. He hopes that the officers will by example, as well as by influence, endeavor to stop it. We can have little hope of the blessing of heaven if we insult God with our speech. . . ." If that note were posted anywhere today, people would fall down laughing.

When you use God's name in vain, all it does is to damn your soul. Someday, everyone will stand before the Judge of all judges, Almighty God, and give an account for how he or she treated His name.

—JOHN HAGEE
Life Lessons to Live By

How do the words you speak bring glory to God?

June 15

The LORD is near to those who have a broken heart,
And saves such as have a contrite spirit.
Many are the afflictions of the righteous,
But the LORD delivers him out of them all.

PSALM 34:18–19

*S*omeone really loves you are words that each of us wants to hear when we have been disappointed and our hearts have been broken. God loves us with an everlasting love, and when life seems impossible, He is always near to comfort, strengthen, and walk with us through whatever disappointments we may face. The Lord will never leave us. Open your heart and let the love of God flow over and through you.

—JACK COUNTRYMAN
Time with God for Mothers

Do you lean on God's everlasting love in hard times, or do you rely on your own strength, or even the comfort of another, to make it through the day?

_____

_____

_____

_____

_____

_____

_____

_____

_____

_____

June 16

The joy of the LORD is your strength.
NEHEMIAH 8:10

One of the characteristics of the Christian is an inward joy that does not depend upon circumstances.

S. D. Gordon, said of joy: "Joy is distinctly a Christian word and a Christian thing. It is the reverse of happiness. Happiness is the result of what happens of an agreeable sort. Joy has its springs deep down inside. And that spring never runs dry, no matter what happens." Only Jesus gives that joy.

—BILLY GRAHAM
Peace with God

As the people of Israel celebrated the feast of trumpets, what do you have to celebrate and give thanks for today?

_____

_____

_____

_____

_____

_____

_____

_____

_____

_____

_____

_____

June 17

I can do all things through Christ who strengthens me.
PHILIPPIANS 4:13

Do you ever find yourself questioning whether you are strong enough or capable enough to handle the responsibilities that God has placed in your hands?

When you begin to wonder if you're up to the challenge, remember that God has prepared you for what He has given you to do. All through your childhood and young adult years, like a potter with fresh clay on the wheel, He molded and shaped your character, equipping you for what is ahead. He has prepared you in ways you never imagined in order for you to fulfill the purpose He has for your life.

So relax. Whatever God's called you to do, you can do it—and you won't have to do it alone.

God's Daily Answer

What current goal in life are you struggling with and questioning your ability to accomplish?

_____

_____

_____

_____

_____

_____

_____

_____

June 18

Of His fullness we have all received,
and grace for grace.
JOHN 1:16

As children of God, we are the primary recipients of His blessing. When the Mediterranean Sea evaporates or runs low, the Atlantic Ocean rushes in at the Strait of Gibraltar to replenish it and keep it full. When you and I are related to Jesus Christ, our strength and wisdom and peace and joy and hope may run out, but His life rushes in to keep us filled to the brim.

—ANNE GRAHAM LOTZ
Just Give Me Jesus

When was the last time you thanked God for His abundant grace? Do so today!

June 19

Knowing that you were not redeemed with corruptible things,
like silver or gold, . . . but with the blood of Christ, as of a
lamb without blemish and without spot.
1 PETER 1:18–19

When Solomon dedicated the temple and slaughtered 22,000 bulls and 120,000 sheep, the blood ran down the altar (2 Chronicles 7:5). But that blood will not redeem you. Even the blood of the apostle Paul, who was martyred for his faith in Christ, does not redeem. The only blood that can remove the crimson stain of sin is the precious blood of the Lamb of God.

Look at Him at the Cross, with heaven and earth watching. He bleeds His life away—from His head, His hands, His feet. That blood gives you spiritual freedom. . . . It was for you, for me, and for the world that we might have everlasting life.

—JOHN HAGEE
Life Lessons to Live By

Take a moment to thank Jesus for His blood that He shed to cleanse you from
your sins.

June 20

His compassions fail not.
They are new every morning;
Great is Your faithfulness.
LAMENTATIONS 3:22–23

Some of us know very little of suffering, but we know disappointments and betrayals and losses and bitterness. Are we really meant to thank God for such things? Let's be clear about one thing. God does not cause all the things we don't like. But He does permit them to happen because it is in this fallen world that we humans must learn to walk by faith. He doesn't leave us to ourselves, however. He shares every step.

—ELISABETH ELLIOT
Keep a Quiet Heart

When was the last time you had a chance to share God's compassion with someone who is suffering?

_____

_____

_____

_____

_____

_____

_____

_____

_____

_____

June 21

Be of good comfort, be of one mind,
live in peace; and the God of love and
peace will be with you.
2 CORINTHIANS 13:11

Marriage is a holy bond because it permits two people to help each other work out their spiritual destinies. God declared marriage to be good because He knew that man needed a helpmate and woman needed a protector. He desires that husbands and wives never lose sight of the original purpose of marriage. It is woman's role to love and help and reassure her husband in every way she can, and it is man's role to love and protect and provide for his wife and the children she bears, so that the home may be filled with God's peace and harmony.

—BILLY GRAHAM
Peace with God

Pray for God's blessings and protection for marriages—your own, your parents', and your friends'.

_____

_____

_____

_____

_____

_____

_____

_____

_____

June 22

It is written, "Man shall not live by bread alone,
but by every word of God."

LUKE 4:4

There is one common problem people have with the Word of God: they don't read it. No other literature will lead you into paths of righteousness.

Jesus compared the Word of God to daily bread. Now bread has to be eaten to do you any good. You can know everything about the loaf that is sitting on your table, but if you don't eat it, it won't help you. And the fact is: you are what you eat. Ezekiel was instructed by God, "open your mouth and eat what I give you" (Ezekiel 2:8). We must bring the Word of God into our lives and make it a part of our soul.

—JOHN HAGEE
Life Lessons to Live By

Do you see the Word of God as your source of life, your daily bread? Or is it your weekly, monthly, or New Year's resolution that lasts only two weeks bread?

June 23

Good people will be guided by honesty;
dishonesty will destroy those who are not trustworthy.
PROVERBS 11:3 NCV

Charles Swindoll correctly observed, "Nothing speaks louder or more powerfully than a life of integrity." Godly men and women agree. Integrity is built slowly over a lifetime. It is a precious thing—difficult to build but easy to tear down. As believers in Christ, we must seek to live each day with discipline, honesty, and faith. When we do, at least two things happen: integrity becomes a habit, and God blesses us because of our obedience to Him.

Living a life of integrity isn't always the easiest way, but it is always the right way. And God clearly intends that it should be our way too.

—CRISWELL FREEMAN
Purpose for Everyday Living

What decisions have you made to ensure that no one will ever question your integrity?

June 24

The Lord is near to all who call upon Him,
To all who call upon Him in truth.
He will fulfill the desire of those who fear Him;
He will also hear their cry and save them.
PSALM 145:18–19

Worry is a killer in the spiritual life of a Christian. When worry walks in your door, doubt will soon follow. God is the great Provider. Do not look to God merely hoping for what you need, but rather look to Him *expecting* what you need. Put your hope in His great love, and worry will eventually disappear as you take your concerns to God, who has the power and wisdom to take care of them.

—JACK COUNTRYMAN
Time with God for Fathers

Do you trust that He always has your best interest at heart? If so, explain.

*Suffering produces perseverance;
perseverance, character; and character, hope.*
ROMANS 5:3–4 NIV

Children find it difficult to wait for anything. They live in a world of microwave popcorn, instant soup, and cartoons on demand. Yet, as an adult, you know that the enduring things of life seldom come without delay, hard work, and perseverance. Your education took years of study. Your profession involves long hours of concentration and effort. And marriage and raising a family require time, patience, wisdom, and a long-term commitment.

Knowing these things doesn't mean that you always like the waiting and the persevering—like children, you, too, sometimes want to see instant results. But when you feel impatient or frustrated, remember the benefits of perseverance.

God's Daily Answer

Are you currently going through trials? Do you still hold on to this hope and promise that God is working in you, making you holy?

June 26

I will praise the LORD according to his righteousness: and
will sing praise to the name of the LORD most high.
PSALM 7:17 KJV

David was called the sweet singer of Israel, and his praising God was called glorifying God. "I will praise thee, O Lord my God, with all my heart; and I will glorify thy name evermore" (Psalm 86:12). Though nothing can add to God's essential glory, praise exalts him in the eyes of others. When we praise God, we spread his fame and renown, we display the trophies of his excellence. In this manner the angels glorify him; they are the choristers of heaven, and do trumpet forth his praise.

Praising God is one of the highest and purest acts. . . . In prayer we act like men; in praise we act like angels.

—THOMAS WATSON
A Body of Divinity

Write words of praise to the Father, then read them out loud with heartfelt joy!

June 27

If you abide in Me, and My words
abide in you, ask whatever you wish,
and it will be done for you.
JOHN 15:7 NASB

This "abide in Me" is the all-inclusive condition for effective intercession. It is the key for prayer in the name of Jesus. . . . As we live this way, we develop what Thomas à Kempis calls "a familiar friendship with Jesus." We become accustomed to His face. We distinguish the voice of the true Shepherd from that of religious hucksters in the same way professional jewelers distinguish a diamond from glass imitations—by acquaintanceship. When we have been around the genuine article long enough, the cheap and the shoddy become obvious.

—RICHARD J. FOSTER
Prayer: Finding the Heart's True Home

What must you do to abide in Jesus and for His words to abide in you?

June 28

If you endure chastening, God deals with you as with sons;
for what son is there whom a father does not chasten?
HEBREWS 12:7

It's a fundamental truth that God loves you too much to leave you as you are. He will therefore work in your life and in your heart to make you more like Christ.

The word *chastening* reflects this truth. The Greek translation means "correction, discipline, training, and nurturing, with the goal of improving one's character." Just as our human parents corrected us because they loved us, our heavenly Father will reprove and discipline us because He loves us. When He sees us straying from His path, He will not sit by idly and watch. When He sees us falling into sin, He will not ignore it. When He sees us getting lazy in our devotions, He will allow us to suffer the consequences. He will love us with persistent and transforming love. That's what a loving parent does.

—HENRY AND RICHARD BLACKABY
Discovering God's Daily Agenda

In what ways have you given the Lord opportunity to chasten, or love, you?

June 29

Then he showed me Joshua the high priest standing before the Angel of the
Lord, and Satan standing at his right hand to oppose him. And the Lord said
to Satan, "The Lord rebuke you, Satan! The Lord who has chosen Jerusalem
rebuke you! Is this not a brand plucked from the fire?"

ZECHARIAH 3:1–2

The Bible is clear that there is a real devil who slithered into the Garden of Eden and seduced Adam and Eve (Genesis 3). The same devil tempted Jesus in the wilderness (Matthew 4). Satan and his angels were cast out of heaven and deceive the world (Revelation 12:9). He is the father of lies (John 8:44) and the accuser of the brethren (Revelation 12:10). Paul says Satan is the "prince of the power of the air, the spirit who now works in the sons of disobedience" (Ephesians 2:2). Behind every temptation, there is the tempter. Behind every lie, there is the father of lies. Behind every murder, there is Satan who was "a murderer from the beginning" (John 8:44).

Jesus taught us to pray, "Deliver us from the evil one" (Matthew 6:13). God has the power and authority to set you free from darkness. Jesus said, "Therefore if the Son makes you free, you shall be free indeed" (John 8:36). Satan was utterly defeated by Christ at Calvary and through his resurrection.

—JOHN HAGEE
Life Lessons to Live By

Do you believe in Satan, or is he a fictional character to you? If you believe in him, do
you fear him, or do you trust in the power of Christ in your life?

_____

_____

_____

June 30

As many of you as were
baptized into Christ have put on Christ.
GALATIANS 3:27

You read it right. We have "put on" Christ. When God looks at us He doesn't see us; He sees Christ. We "wear" Him. We are hidden in Him; we are covered by Him. As the song says "Dressed in His righteousness alone, faultless to stand before the throne."

Presumptuous, you say? Sacrilegious? It would be if it were my idea. But it isn't; it's His.

—MAX LUCADO
He Chose the Nails

Write down what this verse means to you as a Christian.

_____

_____

_____

_____

_____

_____

_____

_____

_____

_____

_____

_____

_____

July

Faith is not belief without proof
but trust without reservation.
D. ELTON TRUEBLOOD

July 1

Every branch that bears fruit He prunes,
that it may bear more fruit.
JOHN 15:2

Submitting to God's pruning can be painful. Yielding requires persistent faith. We must hold tightly to God's character with tears in our eyes.

But our Master Gardener is trustworthy. He loves us too much to elevate looking good above being good. With each cut of His "pruning knife," God thins our lives in order to thicken our character.

—ALICIA BRITT CHOLE
Pure Joy

How much fruit do you plan on harvesting for God in the coming year?

_____

_____

_____

_____

_____

_____

_____

_____

_____

_____

July 2

*A man can do nothing better than to eat and drink and find
satisfaction in his work. This too, I see, is from the hand of God,
for without him, who can eat or find enjoyment?*
ECCLESIASTES 2:24–25 NIV

Are you giving work your best shot? Or are you tending to do what you can to get by? One thing for sure . . . we live in a culture that doesn't glorify laziness. And although we can let work get out of hand, laziness is not a quality that God admires either. He wants us to do what we do with all our might, because laziness will allow our life to pass by without ever experiencing significant accomplishment.

You may not be that happy in your job, but remember, fulfillment and purpose in your work will not come apart from God. When we work to please ourselves or the people around us more than God, we will always be controlled by the successes and failures that our work produces. When we work to please God, we find that He gives us direction and a sense of meaning even when it's hard—even when our talent is underutilized.

—BRYANT WRIGHT
Right from the Heart

*What can you change—in attitude or in actions—so that you are working to please
God and not man?*

July 3

*Work out your own
salvation with fear and trembling.*
PHILIPPIANS 2:12

It would have been nice if God had let us order life like we order a meal. I'll take good health and a high IQ. I'll pass on the music skills, but give me a fast metabolism. . . . Would've been nice. But it didn't happen. When it came to your life on earth, you weren't given a voice or a vote.

But when it comes to life after death, you were. In my book that seems like a good deal. Wouldn't you agree?

—MAX LUCADO
He Chose the Nails

What steps have you taken to work out your salvation each day?

_____

_____

_____

_____

_____

_____

_____

_____

_____

_____

_____

July 4

*God did not send His Son into the world
to condemn the world, but that the world through Him might be saved.*
JOHN 3:17

The word "benevolence" is derived from the combination of the Latin prefix *bene*, which means "well" or "good," and the Latin root that means "will." Together the prefix and the root mean "goodwill."

The Incarnation was an expression of the goodwill of God. His benevolent love. Christ came into the world not only by the will of the Father but by the goodwill of the Father.

—R. C. SPROUL
Loved by God

What friends do you have who need to know the Lord? Pray for each one today.

July 5

*Immediately Jesus made his disciples get into the boat and go
on ahead of him to Bethsaida, while he dismissed the crowd.
After leaving them, he went up on a mountainside to pray.*
MARK 6:45–46 NIV

He was exhausted, completely worn out from dealing with people and
their problems. What He needed was a rest. He got away to spend some
time alone with God. When He did, His spirit was renewed and refreshed.
When the crowds came, He was able to respond, to care for them, and meet
their needs.

His name was Jesus Christ and He was the busiest man who ever lived. He
accomplished more than anyone did before or since His time here.

We live in a very fast-paced world with great demands on our time, yet
no one has ever been busier than Jesus when He walked on this earth. Why
not learn from Him when you're frazzled, exhausted, and burned out. Daily
take some time to be with God. If Jesus needed some time alone with God,
surely we do as well.

—BRYANT WRIGHT
Right from the Heart

*List below some of the things in life that have you frazzled. Take time, as much time
as you need, to pray over these things, asking God for renewal and rest.*

_____

_____

_____

_____

_____

July 6

Test all things; hold fast what is good. Abstain from every form of evil.
1 THESSALONIANS 5:21–22

When we seek righteousness in our own lives—and when we seek the companionship of those who do likewise—we reap the spiritual rewards that God intends for us to enjoy. When we live righteously and according to God's commandments, He blesses us in ways that we cannot fully understand.

Today, as you fulfill your responsibilities, hold fast that which is good, and associate yourself with believers who behave themselves in like fashion. When you do, your good works will serve as a powerful example for others and as a worthy offering to your Creator.

—CRISWELL FREEMAN
Purpose for Everyday Living

When you became a Christian, did your friendships change? Have you chosen to be associated with those of like faith? If so, how has that helped your Christian walk?

July 7

He who trusts in his riches will fall,
But the righteous will flourish like foliage.
PROVERBS 11:28

We come into life with empty hands—and it is with empty hands that we leave it. Actually we can possess nothing—no property and no person—along the way. It is God who owns everything, and we are but stewards of His property during the brief time we are on earth. Everything that we see about us that we count as our possessions only comprises a loan from God.

—BILLY GRAHAM
Peace with God

What legacy do you plan to leave for your family?

_____

_____

_____

_____

_____

_____

_____

_____

_____

_____

_____

July 8

*Yet who knows whether you have come
to the kingdom for such a time as this?*
ESTHER 4:14

God chose to give Esther significant and far-reaching influence as He turned ordinary events (King Ahasuerus looking for a bride) into extraordinary opportunities to achieve His purposes (saving the Jewish people from extermination). Because of Esther's virtue and courage, God used her to save the lives of thousands of her countrymen and to change the course of history.

Just as God prepared Esther, He is preparing you for His next assignment for you. Each step of faithfulness prepares you for what awaits. God will use your current circumstances for His next great work in and through your life.

—HENRY AND RICHARD BLACKABY
Discovering God's Daily Agenda

Has God placed you in a position of influence—over your household, over someone at work, over a ministry in your church? Think and pray about how and why this is, and ask God to continue using your circumstances to further His kingdom.

July 9

Now He who establishes us with you in Christ and has anointed us is God,
who also has sealed us and given us the Spirit in our hearts as a guarantee.
2 CORINTHIANS 1:21–22

You need insurance when you don't have assurance. Without the assurance that other drivers will obey the traffic laws, you need car insurance. Without the assurance that a fire won't ignite in your home, you need homeowner's insurance. You purchase insurance, just in case.

But, when it comes to God, there is no need for a backup plan. You have the assurance that God will never fail. Never. Read the stories of Abraham and Moses in the Old Testament. Take note of how God never failed to come through—even when those who promised to faithfully follow Him did not.

God's Daily Answer

Can you recall some times in your life that God came through for you, even if you gave up hope in Him?

_____

_____

_____

_____

_____

_____

_____

_____

_____

_____

July 10

Great is our Lord, and mighty in power;
His understanding is infinite.
PSALM 147:5

No means of measure can define God's limitless love. No barrier can hinder Him from pouring out His blessings.

He forgives and He forgets. He creates and He cleanses.

He restores and He rebuilds. He comforts and He carries.

He lifts and He loves. He is the God of the second chance.

—ANNE GRAHAM LOTZ
Just Give Me Jesus

What comfort does this verse give you today?

July 11

The eyes of the LORD are in every place,
Keeping watch on the evil and the good.
PROVERBS 15:3

The thought that someone is watching seldom occurs to us as we go through life. So often, we say what we want and do exactly what we self-ishly choose to do. We need to realize that nothing ever escapes the notice of God and nothing ever surprises Him. When we commit our ways to the Lord, everything changes, and pleasing God becomes our priority in life. Because God cares, He wants to bless us with His love and mercy.

—JACK COUNTRYMAN
Time with God for Fathers

Does your life reflect the love and mercy God so generously gives to you?

_____

_____

_____

_____

_____

_____

_____

_____

_____

_____

July 12

Having been justified by faith,
we have peace with God.
ROMANS 5:1

Many of us have entered the Christian life by faith. But having entered, we are inclined to shift our ground. We come to feel that we will become righteous (that is, remain acceptable to God) only as we do certain things.

Yet with a concerted voice, the New Testament writers teach that God's supreme interest is in what we are, not what we do.

—CATHERINE MARSHALL
Moments that Matter

In your own words, explain why you are at peace with God.

July 13

Who is the man that fears the LORD?
Him shall He teach in the way He chooses.
PSALM 25:12

It's not fair," we say. It's not fair that I was born in poverty or that I sing so poorly or that I run so slowly. But the scales of life were forever tipped on the side of fairness when God planted a tree in the Garden of Eden. All complaints were silenced when Adam and his descendants were given free will, the freedom to make whatever eternal choice we desire. Any injustice in this life is offset by the honor of choosing our destiny in the next.

—MAX LUCADO
He Chose the Nails

When you see the words "fears the LORD," what thoughts come to your mind?

July 14

*The Helper, the Holy Spirit, whom
the Father will send in My name, He will teach you all
things, and bring to your remembrance
all things that I said to you.*
JOHN 14:26

Today, many agree on what is absolutely evil and absolutely good. But in a world of ever-expanding shades of gray, we can lose confidence in our ability to distinguish where light ends and darkness begins.

Yet God always sees clearly. When faced with a specific decision, let us first look to His Word and ask a simple question: Can I picture God smiling over this choice?

God's Spirit will be faithful to teach us and guide us into all truth.

—ALICIA BRITT CHOLE
Pure Joy

How often do you ask the Holy Spirit to guide you when any decision needs to be made?

July 15

Let a man so consider us, as servants
of Christ and stewards of the mysteries of God.
Moreover it is required in stewards
that one be found faithful.
1 CORINTHIANS 4:1–2

Christ is the grand over-comer. By receiving Jesus into our lives, we erect the inner bracing that enables us to withstand the pressure of all our outer circumstances. Welcoming Christ into our lives, we gain the power to control life and not be crushed by it. Yet to withstand the crush of life, we must always be submitted to His inner lordship. The yielded life becomes the strong life.

—CALVIN MILLER
Into the Depths of God

If you are a servant of Christ, how would you be found faithful?

_____

_____

_____

_____

_____

_____

_____

_____

_____

July 16

He bruises, but He binds up;
He wounds, but His hands make whole.
JOB 5:18

Oh, the hands of Jesus. Hands of incarnation at His birth. Hands of liberation as He healed. Hands of inspiration as He taught. Hands of dedication as He served. And hands of salvation as He died.

The same hand that stilled the seas stills your guilt.

The same hand that cleansed the Temple cleanses your heart.

The hand is the hand of God.

—MAX LUCADO
He Chose the Nails

When you have been wounded, what steps have you taken to heal your wounds?

July 17

He has made His wonderful works to be remembered;
The Lord is gracious and full of compassion.
PSALM 111:4

Life brings disappointment, disease, despair, and death. No one walks this journey without encountering rocky roads. Often life seems terribly unfair and inexplicable. Yesterday, friends of mine lost their baby, less than twenty-four hours old. Why? They would have made wonderful parents, and they longed for this baby and prayed for him for years. Now he's gone, and their arms are empty.

At a time like this, the most important reality is God's sovereignty. Chuck Swindoll says, "God is not *almost* sovereign. He is in complete control of the circumstances of our lives. He is good. And He is full of mercy." He sees what we can't, knows what we don't, can do the impossible, and He is good. All of that, all the time. So we trust Him. In His greatest act of sovereignty and kindness to us all, He provided a Savior to forgive our sin.

—MARY GRAHAM
Women of Faith Devotional Bible

Write a prayer acknowledging God's sovereignty over a difficult situation in your life.

_____

_____

_____

_____

_____

_____

_____

July 18

Blessed are those who keep His testimonies,
Who seek Him with the whole heart!
PSALM 119:2

Have you ever thought of going to church as a divine appointment? Have you ever thought of Bible study as a divine appointment? That Jesus is patiently, personally waiting to meet with you there?

What a difference it would make in our attitude of expectancy and our habit of consistency if we truly wrapped our hearts around the knowledge that each is a divine appointment; that Jesus Himself is waiting to meet with us.

—ANNE GRAHAM LOTZ
Just Give Me Jesus

What steps are you taking to seek the Lord with all your heart?

July 19

Well done, good and faithful servant;
you were faithful over a few things, I will
make you ruler over many things.
MATTHEW 25:21

The Cross is a sign of loss—a shameful, humiliating, abject, total loss. Yet it was Jesus' loss that meant heavenly gain for the whole world. Although secured in a tomb with a heavy stone, a seal, and posted guards, He could not be held down by death. He came out of the grave as the Death of Death and Hell's Destruction. His death was a new beginning. Those who accept that truth receive not only the promise of heaven, but the possibility of heaven on earth, where the Risen Christ walks with us.

—ELISABETH ELLIOT
Keep a Quiet Heart

What needs to happen in your life for the Lord to say, "well done, good and faithful servant"?

_____

_____

_____

_____

_____

_____

_____

_____

_____

July 20

The joy of the LORD is your strength.
NEHEMIAH 8:10

O ne sign of spiritual starvation is exhaustion. If there is no joy, there is no strength, and exhaustion sets in. That exhaustion, if not remedied, leads to depression. A joyless Christian is always a defeated, depressed Christian. You need a joy explosion. When you read God's Word, may God's joy leap from the page and strengthen your soul. The Word of God says we are soldiers in the army of God, and the command is to fight the good fight of faith. The victory is ours through Christ the Lord.

If we lose our joy, we lose our Christian credibility. "If you faint in the day of adversity, your strength is small" (Proverbs 24:10). Daily begin to read the Word of God slowly and prayerfully, and joy will be restored in your soul.

—JOHN HAGEE
Life Lessons to Live By

Do you feel God's strength in your life, or are you exhausted and depressed? Feast on God's Word, realize His love for you, and feel strength rise as His joy flows through you.

July 21

Wise men turn away wrath.
PROVERBS 29:8

Your temper is either your master or your servant. Either you control it, or it controls you. And the extent to which you allow anger to rule your life will determine, to a surprising extent, the quality of your relationships with others and your relationship with God.

Anger and peace cannot coexist in the same mind. If you allow yourself to be chronically angry, you must forfeit, albeit temporarily, the peace that might otherwise be yours through Christ. So obey God's Word by turning away from anger today.

—CRISWELL FREEMAN
Purpose for Everyday Living

Find a verse that will inspire a godly response the next time you are faced with getting angry. Write it below and commit it to memory.

_____

_____

_____

_____

_____

_____

_____

_____

_____

_____

July 22

Repent therefore and be converted, that your sins may be blotted out, so that times of refreshing may come from the presence of the Lord.

ACTS 3:19

When physical infection is caused by a virus, doctors treat symptoms. When the contamination is spiritual and the result of sin, God doesn't just deal with symptoms; He deals with the cause and brings healing. He expects us to eradicate sin and its causes from our lives.

So be proactive about sin. Everything and everyone you touch becomes contaminated when sin renders you unclean, so it is imperative that you guard your purity—with the protection of God's Word, the power of His Spirit, and the fellowship with His people.

—HENRY AND RICHARD BLACKABY
Discovering God's Daily Agenda

Pray a prayer of repentance for any sins weighing on your heart. Afterward, write all the ways you feel "refreshed" by the power of His Spirit.

_____

_____

_____

_____

_____

_____

_____

_____

_____

July 23

Where can I flee from Your presence? . . .
If I take the wings of the morning,
And dwell in the uttermost parts of the sea,
Even there Your hand shall lead me.
PSALM 139:7, 9–10

O ur asking "Where is God?" is like a fish asking "Where is water?" or a bird asking "Where is air?" God is everywhere! Equally present in Peking and Peoria. As active in the lives of Icelanders as in the lives of Texans. We cannot find a place where God is not.

—MAX LUCADO
He Chose the Nails

If God is available and everywhere, what steps have you taken to take His hand to lead you?

_____

_____

_____

_____

_____

_____

_____

_____

_____

_____

_____

July 24

Blessed are they that mourn: for they shall be comforted.
MATTHEW 5:4 KJV

Where do you turn when you find yourself anxious, worried, discouraged, or in pain? There is an endless list of "comforters" people like to turn to—television, sports, shopping, food. But, God is the only comforter who does more than cover up the uncomfortable. God's comfort also heals.

Whatever grieves your heart grieves the heart of the One who loves you. Turning your worries into prayers allows God to put His arms around you, often in unexpected ways. Whether you find God's comfort in renewed peace of mind, joy in His creation, or companionship from someone God's placed in your life, let God soothe your soul today in ways that comfort food and mindless distractions never will.

God's Daily Answer

What have you found to be the best way to solve life's daily problems? Have you included God in your solution?

July 25

The Son of Man has come to seek and to save that which was lost.
LUKE 19:10

You can tell how much I value something by the effort I put into finding it. If I lose a paperclip on my desk, I only look for a second before grabbing another one. But if I lose my wallet, I won't rest until it's recovered. Did you know there's a way to measure how much God values us? The Bible says He loves us so much that He sent His only Son to earth to find us. Think of that—God giving His Son because you and I were lost. Nothing makes me feel so valuable as knowing what God did to find me. God values you, too, more than you might realize. Remember He would have sent His Son to the cross even if you were the only person on earth. Wow! Amazing love.

—DAVID JEREMIAH
1 Minute a Day

Have you ever stopped and realized the great lengths that God went to just to find and rescue you? When you think about it, how does that make you feel? Special? Loved?

July 26

"Surely I am coming quickly."
Amen. Even so, come, Lord Jesus!
REVELATION 22:20

The Lord Jesus is coming back! That's how much He loves us. The plan of salvation is not only to satisfy us in this world and give us a new life here, but He has a great plan for the future. For eternity!

—BILLY GRAHAM
Peace with God

The Lord Jesus is coming back. Are you ready for His coming?

July 27

Call to Me, and I will answer you, and show you
great and mighty things, which you do not know.
JEREMIAH 33:3

My mother spoke to me about prayer in these terms: "Some prayer, some power. More prayer, more power. Much prayer, much power." Add to that these words from Martyn Lloyd-Jones: "Man is at his greatest and highest when upon his knees he comes face-to-face with God." You have as much or as little of God's power in your life as you're willing to pray to receive. "God is no respecter of persons" (Acts 10:34 KJV).

When you come to our Almighty God, you come to the God who loves you as your Father. He can make a way when there seems no way, and He cannot fail. He will plant you by rivers of water (Psalm 1:3). The new opportunity that is right in front of you, He can cause to explode with possibilities.

—JOHN HAGEE
Life Lessons to Live By

Are you in the habit of praying, or do you only pray when things go downhill? Why not invite the Almighty God into your life every day to give you the strength and power to face anything.

July 28

Give us this day our daily bread.
MATTHEW 6:11

Jesus invites us to pray for daily bread.

In doing so, He has transfigured the trivialities of everyday life. Try to imagine what our prayer experience would be like if He had forbidden us to ask for the little things. What if the only things we were allowed to talk about were the weighty matters, the important things, the profound issues? We would be orphaned in the cosmos, cold, and terribly alone. But the opposite is true; He welcomes us with our 1,001 trifles, for they are each important to Him.

—RICHARD J. FOSTER
Prayer: Finding the Heart's True Home

What kind of a prayer experience are you having with the Lord each day?

July 29

I will strengthen you,
Yes, I will help you.
I will uphold you with my righteous right hand.
ISAIAH 41:10

Whatever the circumstances, whatever the call, whatever the duty, whatever the price, whatever the sacrifice—God's strength will be your strength in your hour of need.

—BILLY GRAHAM
Peace with God

What promises of encouragement come from this verse?

_____

_____

_____

_____

_____

_____

_____

_____

_____

_____

_____

_____

_____

July 30

Death and life are in the power of the tongue,
And those who love it will eat its fruit.
PROVERBS 18:21

Have you ever considered the impact your words have on your children and those you love? Your words can either build up or destroy their confidence. Your children look to you for love, guidance, and how to cope with growing up in today's world. Choose carefully the words you speak, because the impression you make will greatly impact who your children become.

—JACK COUNTRYMAN
Time with God for Fathers

List some specific words you can say to your children that will build them up. Look for opportune times to say them, and then do!

July 31

Let all that you do be done with love.
1 CORINTHIANS 16:14

Who wants to be around someone who is critical? I don't see any raised hands out there. A critical spirit is constricting, cruel, and caustic. And being critical of others is as habit-forming as nicotine and caffeine, and it stifles the music in our hearts. When I'm critical, that's often a warning that I'm too busy, too tired, and too self-absorbed.

So how can we have a melody restored?

Ask the Lord to give us a new song, a toe-tapping song of praise.

Practice praising others. Not empty words of someone trying too hard to impress, but sincere words of truth so they fit into the hearer's heart.

—PATSY CLAIRMONT
The Hat Box

Ask the Lord to give you a new song in your heart, then list the names of three people whom you can encourage with praise today.

_____

_____

_____

_____

_____

_____

_____

August

*There is a delicious gladness
that comes from God.*
MAX LUCADO

August 1

Those who wait on the LORD
Shall renew their strength;
They shall mount up with wings like eagles.
ISAIAH 40:31

Waiting is part of ordinary time. We discover God in our waiting: waiting in checkout lines, waiting for the telephone to ring, waiting for graduation, waiting for a promotion, waiting to retire, waiting to die. The waiting itself becomes prayer as we give our waiting to God. In waiting we begin to get in touch with the rhythms of life—stillness and action, listening and decision. They are the rhythms of God. It is in the everyday and the commonplace that we learn patience, acceptance, and contentment.

—RICHARD J. FOSTER
Prayer: Finding the Heart's True Home

How hard is it for you to wait upon the Lord?

_____

_____

_____

_____

_____

_____

_____

_____

_____

_____

August 2

For whatever is born of God overcomes the world. And this is the victory that has overcome the world—our faith.

1 JOHN 5:4

The world makes promises that it simply cannot fulfill. It promises happiness, contentment, prosperity, and abundance. But genuine, lasting abundance is not a function of worldly possessions, it is a function of our thoughts, our actions, and the relationship we choose to create with our God. The world's promises are incomplete and illusory; God's promises are unfailing. We must build our lives on the firm foundation of God's promises . . . nothing else will suffice.

—CRISWELL FREEMAN
Purpose for Everyday Living

Have the promises of the world ever been a disappointment in your life? If so, what have you learned and how have you changed from that experience?

August 3

*Present your bodies a living sacrifice, holy,
acceptable to God, which is your reasonable service.*
ROMANS 12:1

The greatest worship you ever render to God is to serve Him. For Paul, service meant a total commitment.

Paul wrote to Timothy, "I thank God, whom I serve with a pure conscience" (2 Timothy 1:3). Paul was saying that you could look deep inside him and see that he served God with his entire being. Paul's service was an act of worship. It was deep, genuine, and honest. That is the real measure of true spirituality. The only way to serve God is with total commitment.

—JOHN MACARTHUR
Truth for Today

In what ways are you serving (or worshiping) God right now? In what ways would you like to serve but aren't? Pray for opportunities that will lead you into more genuine worship.

August 4

Do not be rash with your mouth,
And let not your heart utter anything hastily before God.
For God is in heaven, and you on earth;
Therefore let your words be few.
ECCLESIASTES 5:2

Waiting upon the Lord and listening to Him are foundational to our relationship with Him. It is wonderful to offer God our praise and to express our needs, but to leave His presence before He speaks is a travesty.

In Ecclesiastes, King Solomon concluded that our search for significance and meaning is in vain until we seek God. Only when we go before Him do we, His creatures, gain His wisdom. Humbled, we are to enter God's presence to receive a word from Him, not to ask Him to do our bidding. We are to adjust to His will, not ask Him to bless ours.

—HENRY AND RICHARD BLACKABY
Discovering God's Daily Agenda

What are you are asking God to bless rather than waiting on Him to answer? The next time you pray, allow time to be silent and wait for God to speak.

August 5

I, the LORD, have called You in righteousness,
And will hold Your hand.
ISAIAH 42:6

A re you filled with anxiety and worry about some problem, wondering what will happen? Listen: As a child of God through faith in Christ, you can turn these over to Christ, knowing that He loves you and is able to help you. At times He may take the problem away; other times He may give you strength to bear it. But you can rest in Him.

—BILLY GRAHAM
The Secret of Happiness

Write out your prayer for the heaviest burden on your heart.

_____

_____

_____

_____

_____

_____

_____

_____

_____

_____

_____

August 6

Love your enemies, bless those who curse you,
do good to those who hate you.
MATTHEW 5:44

When Jesus commands us to love our enemies, He defines that love not so much in terms of feelings of affection but in terms of actions. To love our enemies requires that we bless them when they curse us and do good to them when they hate us. This is what it means to mirror and reflect the love of God, because God does good to those who hate Him and blesses people while they are cursing Him.

—R. C. SPROUL
Loved by God

What kind of attitude have you chosen for those you consider as enemies? Have you prayed for them recently?

August 7

*We are made holy through the sacrifice
of the body of Jesus Christ once for all.*
HEBREWS 10:10 NIV

The Son of God became the Lamb of God, the cross became the altar, and we were made holy through the sacrifice Christ made in His body once and for all time.

What needed to be paid was paid. What had to be done was done. Innocent blood was required. Innocent blood was offered, once and for all time. Bury those five words deep in your heart. Once and for all time.

—MAX LUCADO
He Chose the Nails

What have you learned about the sacrifice of Christ from this verse?

_____

_____

_____

_____

_____

_____

_____

_____

_____

_____

_____

_____

August 8

You will keep him in perfect peace
Whose mind is stayed on You,
Because he trusts in You.
ISAIAH 26:3–4

In a world that stands on the brink of wars and rumors of wars and the possibility of our cities being targeted for terrorist attacks, the question is being asked, "Where can we find peace?" Peace . . . the inner tranquility that lets me lie down at night and sleep soundly without worrying about anything. Peace . . . the hope that keeps me expecting all good things to happen. Peace . . . the assurance of knowing even if bad things happen, God has worked it all out for my good.

Peace is a possibility. In fact, God gave us peace. Peace is a promise from Jesus. Peace is a gift from the Holy Spirit. Jesus declared the Comforter, the Holy Spirit, would come to live in the hearts of the people when they received Him as Lord and Savior. The fruit of the Holy Spirit takes up residence in our hearts and brings with Him all His attributes, including peace.

—THELMA WELLS
Women of Faith Devotional Bible

How do you define peace?

August 9

I am the good shepherd; and
I know My sheep, and am known by My own.
JOHN 10:14

Jesus looked out at the approaching crowds and saw people who were seeking God. He saw people as more important than His own plans and need for rest. He saw people not as an interruption, but as an opportunity to reveal His loving care and His Father's compassionate power to meet their deepest needs.

He saw people as sheep who needed a shepherd. He saw people as God saw them.

—ANNE GRAHAM LOTZ
Just Give Me Jesus

How well acquainted are you with the Good Shepherd? Explain.

_____

_____

_____

_____

_____

_____

_____

_____

_____

_____

August 10

Looking unto Jesus, the author
and finisher of our faith . . .
HEBREWS 12:2

Jesus is Lord, and this is the primary positive confession that should define our lives. Humility is our bread, obedience our wine. We gain true humility not by putting ourselves down but by standing next to Christ. Once we see how great is the Savior's love for us, we know our lovely place in the world. Humility thus gained is power and triumph.

—CALVIN MILLER
Into the Depths of God

When trouble walks through your door, whom do you first look to for answers?

August 11

We must not become tired of doing good. Do not give up.
GALATIANS 6:9 NCV

Reaching any goal in life takes more than just hard work. It takes determination. Determination is a mind-set that is constantly evaluating where you are against where you want to be. It not only helps keep you focused on your goal, but on the reasons behind your desire to reach it. It keeps you moving forward, whether your progress is rocky or smooth.

God wants to help. His loving encouragement and perfect perspective are what you need to help you aim high—and not give up.

God's Daily Answer

What objectives, ambitions, or aspirations are you determined to reach in this life? Ask God to help you choose your goals wisely, then move beyond any roadblocks that are slowing your progress.

August 12

Then He went into the temple and began to drive out those who bought and sold in it, saying to them, "It is written, 'My house is a house of prayer,' but you have made it a den of thieves.'"
LUKE 19: 45–46

Why pray? Because prayer changes things! Abraham prayed for a son when he was ninety-nine years old and Sarah was ninety, and God gave him Isaac (Genesis 17:17). Elijah prayed and fire fell from the heavens and consumed the sacrifice, wood, stones, and burned up fifty gallons of water right before the eyes of the prophets of Baal (1 Kings 18:38). The God who answers prayers consistently showed up and demonstrated His power!

On the Day of Pentecost, the Spirit of God came mightily (Acts 2:3). Read the rest of the Book of Acts and you'll see that they turned the world upside down and pulled Rome to its knees by the power of prayer. If you want power with God, learn to pray.

—JOHN HAGEE
Life Lessons to Live By

Do you believe in the power of prayer? Or do you think that miracles don't happen anymore?

August 13

The ones who follow the Lamb . . .
were redeemed from among men.
REVELATION 14:4

We often think of God's will as a thin, barely visible line drawn with chalk that blurs in bad weather. However, the Scriptures speak of our relationship with God as a way, not a line. His will is a path paved with great grace.

God does not play hide-and-seek with those who have committed their lives to Him. Though the specific placement of His children varies greatly, God's will for us all is quite similar. [He] simply says, "follow Me."

—ALICIA BRITT CHOLE
Pure Joy

What does the phrase, "follow Me" mean to you?

_____

_____

_____

_____

_____

_____

_____

_____

_____

_____

_____

August 14

You, O LORD, are our Father;
Our Redeemer from Everlasting.
ISAIAH 63:16

If I am willing to be still in my Master's hand, can I not then be still in everything? He's got the whole world in His hands! Never mind whether things come from God Himself or from people—everything comes by His ordination or permission. If I mean to be obedient and submissive to the Lord because He is my Lord, I must not forget that whatever He allows to happen becomes, for me, His will at that moment.

—ELISABETH ELLIOT
Keep a Quiet Heart

Give thanks today for the many blessings God has given you and praise His
Holy name.

August 15

*All of you who were baptized into Christ
have clothed yourselves with Christ.*
GALATIANS 3:27 NIV

While on the cross, Jesus felt the indignity and disgrace of a criminal. No, He was not guilty. No, He had not committed a sin. And, no, He did not deserve to be sentenced. But you and I were, we had, and we did. Though we come to the cross dressed in sin, we leave the cross dressed in "garments of salvation" (Isaiah 61:10 NIV). Indeed, we leave dressed in Christ Himself.

—MAX LUCADO
He Chose the Nails

What does it mean to you to have clothed yourself with Christ?

August 16

If by one man's offense many died,
much more the grace of God and the gift by the grace
of the one Man, Jesus Christ,
abounded to many.

ROMANS 5:15

We do not come to know God through works—we come to know Him by faith through grace. We cannot work our way toward happiness and heaven; we cannot moralize our way; we cannot reform our way; we cannot buy our way. Salvation comes as a gift of God through Christ.

—BILLY GRAHAM
The Secret of Happiness

How is salvation the greatest of all gifts in your life?

August 17

Every good and perfect gift is from above.
JAMES 1:17 NIV

Not all gifts are given for the right reasons, are they? A gift is to be an expression of love, but sometimes we give out of obligation. Gifts are to be given to bless, but sometimes we give them to impress, don't we?

Not so with God! God is love, and every gift He gives is a perfect expression of His loving nature. He doesn't bless you out of duty. He blesses you because He wants to. He loves you and showers you with gifts of every kind. Spiritual. Physical. Material. Mental. Emotional. Relational. If you were to write a list of God's blessings, it would truly be never-ending, for every breath you take . . . every moment of your life is a gift!

—KARLA DORNACHER
Give Thanks

What is your response to God's gift of life and love to you?

_____

_____

_____

_____

_____

_____

_____

_____

_____

_____

_____

August 18

Do not take revenge, my friends, but leave room for God's wrath, for it is written: "It is mine to avenge; I will repay," says the Lord.
ROMANS 12:19 NIV

Is there anything more satisfying than to have justice delivered to someone who has wronged you? Through a series of betrayals, David's vain young son, Absalom, took away the throne that rightfully belonged to him. David protested and cried out to God for justice but recognized that vengeance is a matter for God. It wasn't long before Absalom—who was very proud of his head of flowing hair—had his gorgeous locks caught in a tree as he was riding by. He couldn't untangle himself and died right there.

God delivers justice in different ways. Sometimes it's through routine personal interaction. Sometimes through normal office procedures. Some actions require the involvement of the police or the courts. And sometimes justice will not be revealed until after our deaths, recognizing that God sees an eternal picture that we cannot comprehend while here on earth. Let's act justly and let Him take care of ultimate justice.

—BRYANT WRIGHT
Right from the Heart

Have you ever had a time in your life when someone betrayed you and you wanted revenge. What was your reaction? Did you turn the problem over to God?

August 19

Every day I will bless You,
And I will praise Your name forever and ever.
Great is the LORD, and greatly to be praised.
PSALM 145:2–3

When life with its twists and turns takes you down unexpected and difficult roads, it can sometimes feel strange to praise the Lord. Yet, He seeks your praise in all things—whether they appear good to us or not. Remember that God is good and always gives ample reason to praise Him. God's overriding purpose for your life is to glorify Him, and He will use any means to accomplish that. Ask Him to open your heart so that you will see your life's circumstances as He does. Despite how you feel, praise can flow from you like a fountain—beginning right now.

—JACK COUNTRYMAN
Time with God for Fathers

What is something you're facing or going through in which it's difficult to praise God? Write it down and take that first step of glorifying Him through praise!

August 20

*Be sober, be vigilant; because your adversary the devil walks about
like a roaring lion, seeking whom he may devour.*
1 PETER 5:8

Because our world is filled with temptations, we confront them at every turn. Some of these temptations are small—eating that second piece of cake, for example. Other temptations, however, are not so harmless.

The devil is hard at work in these difficult days, and as Christians we must remain vigilant. Not only must we resist Satan when he confronts us, but we must also avoid those places where Satan can most easily tempt us. And, we must earnestly wrap ourselves in the protection of God's Holy Word. When we do, we are secure.

—CRISWELL FREEMAN
Purpose for Everyday Living

*Read Ephesians 6:12–18 and write it below. Commit to praying this at the beginning
of every day so that you are able to withstand the devil's schemes.*

August 21

*No prophecy of Scripture is of any private interpretation, for
prophecy never came by the will of man, but holy men of
God spoke as they were moved by the Holy Spirit.*

2 PETER 1:20–21

Do you believe Scripture is perfect truth, is the written Word of God, and is our authority for faith and practice? Or do you believe it contains some general principles written by men that were shaped by prejudices, and exists for each person to do what they feel is right?

Here is the bottom line on the truth of the Scriptures: it is either complete, perfect truth, applicable for all times (through the interpretation of the Holy Spirit), or it is an untrustworthy source filled with lies. There is no in-between. There is no such thing as partial truth or relative truth. The decision you make as to the nature of the Scriptures will shape everything else that you believe about God, about Jesus, about life, and about morality.

—BRYANT WRIGHT
Right from the Heart

*Are there any parts of Scripture you don't believe to be truth? Write the references
here and spend time talking to your pastor or a Bible scholar in order to gain a better
understanding.*

August 22

In everything give thanks; for this is the will
of God in Christ Jesus for you.
1 THESSALONIANS 5:18

How can I deal with resentments that smolder inside me? The verse above holds the answer. I am to praise God for all things, regardless of where they seem to originate. Doing this, He points out, is the key to receiving the blessings of God. Praise will wash away my resentments.

—CATHERINE MARSHALL
Moments that Matter

How hard is it for you to give thanks in everything?

August 23

*Delight yourself also in the L*ORD*,*
And He shall give you the desires of your heart.
PSALM 37:4

Consider this: When you pray, an almighty God is sitting on His throne in heaven, and His hand is cupped behind His ear. He's listening for His children to pray to Him and to ask for great and mighty things, to ask for signs and wonders, to ask for miracles. He's waiting for us to ask Him to pull down the strongholds and powers and principalities that are destroying our lives, the lives of our children, our church, our city, and nation. So what do you ask Him to do?

—JOHN HAGEE
Life Lessons to Live By

Do you ever limit your prayers to things that are feasible—only asking God to meet certain needs that seem more attainable, but leaving out bigger things like ending wars and stopping violence?

August 24

The mind controlled by the Spirit is life and peace.
ROMANS 8:6 NIV

Physically, you are what you eat, but spiritually, you are what you think. If you worry and stew over a situation, looking for your own answers about how to fix a problem, peace will elude you. Instead, when something is bothering you, meditate on the nature of God. He has all the answers. Take a moment to think about His greatness. Then, think about what is right in the world and in your life, rather than what is wrong with it. Contemplate a Scripture, and let its words wash through your mind.

Meditation is about pausing in the midst of your situation and listening to the inner voice of the Holy Spirit. It's like a calm break, designed to give you an opportunity to focus on the One who has the answers.

God's Daily Answer

Write a Scripture verse below that will help you stay focused on the unfailing character of God the next time you're tempted to worry.

August 25

If we live in the Spirit,
let us also walk in the Spirit.
GALATIANS 5:25

The Holy Spirit is powerfully at work in your life, hovering over your heart, preparing you to love God. He hovers over your mind, preparing you to understand spiritual things and the truth of His Word. He hovers over your will, preparing you to make decisions that are pleasing to Him. All the powers of God—the same power that hung the stars in place and put the planets in their courses and transformed Earth—now resides in you to energize and strengthen you to become the person God created you to be.

—ANNE GRAHAM LOTZ
Just Give Me Jesus

How much time do you spend listening to the Holy Spirit to become the person God created you to be?

_____

_____

_____

_____

_____

_____

_____

_____

_____

_____

August 26

A righteous man is cautious in friendship,
but the way of the wicked leads them astray.
PROVERBS 12:26 NIV

People will often wrap themselves in the identity of other people or groups. Some will choose to be identified as Republicans or Democrats, conservationists or environmentalists, or maybe just part of the elite. Many people will embrace the identity of the college they attended and wrap themselves in the colors and excitement of that college, even to the point that their mood for the entire week depends on whether their football team won or lost the previous Saturday. (I wish I didn't battle this disease.)

How about you? Is there someone you have chosen to identify with? Be careful with that decision because the person you become will reflect whomever you choose to follow and/or befriend. And the image that others have of you will reflect those with whom you identify. Knowing that, it only makes sense to choose to be identified with Jesus Christ. Even those who don't follow Him never question His character.

—BRYANT WRIGHT
Right from the Heart

Do your everyday actions indicate that your identity is in your heavenly Father?

August 27

*The peace of God, which surpasses
all understanding, will guard your
hearts and minds through Christ Jesus.*
PHILIPPIANS 4:7

The storm was raging. The sea was beating against the rocks in huge, dashing waves. The lightning was flashing, the thunder was roaring, the wind was blowing; but the little bird was asleep in the crevice of the rock, its head serenely under its wing, sound asleep.

In Christ we are relaxed and at peace in the midst of the confusions, bewilderments, and perplexities of this life. The storm rages, but our hearts are at rest.

—BILLY GRAHAM
Peace with God

When did you recieve the peace of God that "surpasses all understanding"?

_____

_____

_____

_____

_____

_____

_____

_____

_____

_____

August 28

I must work the works of Him who sent Me while it is day;
the night is coming when no one can work.
JOHN 9:4

The words of John 9:4 remind us that "night is coming" for all of us. But until then, God gives us each day and fills it to the brim with possibilities. The day is presented to us fresh and clean at midnight, free of charge, but we must beware: today is a non-renewable resource—once it's gone, it's gone forever. Our responsibility, of course, is to use this day in the service of God's will and in accordance with His commandments. This day is a priceless gift from your Creator, so use it joyfully and productively!

—CRISWELL FREEMAN
Purpose for Everyday Living

Today, what will you change, how will you treasure the time that God has given you?

August 29

On that night God appeared to Solomon,
and said to him, "Ask! What shall I give you?"
2 CHRONICLES 1:7

God Almighty is not a statue. He speaks, talks, thinks, and feels our infirmities. He answers prayer. He's alive. He responds. He's the God who is there. He's there in the night when you ask, "God, where are You?" He answers, "I'm right here! Call upon Me!" He gets excited when you get down on your knees. He says, "Look, here she comes. Here he comes. We're finally going to get to talk. Angels, get ready. We're going to carry the answer back to earth and show them things they've never seen before." Do you need for the impossible to happen? Ask. Nothing is impossible with God.

—JOHN HAGEE
Life Lessons to Live By

How does it make you feel to know that God is sitting by, eagerly waiting on you to open up to Him?

August 30

He will judge the world in righteousness;
he will govern the peoples with justice.
PSALM 9:8 NIV

The judgment of man is very different from the judgment of God. While man focuses on guilt or innocence, God's judgment is so much more. That's because God already knows our guilt from sin. He needs no evidence of that. But what He does want to know is that we acknowledge our sin and offer a willingness to change. He wants us to recognize that our sin has separated us from Him and wants us to express a mourning that cries out for His mercy through faith in what Jesus did on the cross—dying to pay the penalty for our sin. It is only through this process that we can experience God's perfect justice and God's perfect mercy.

—BRYANT WRIGHT
Right from the Heart

Change is often difficult for adults. How have you changed since becoming a Christian?

August 31

Blessed are all those who put their trust in Him.
PSALM 2:12

In the race of life, God our heavenly Father has come alongside us through the Person of the Holy Spirit. And when we think we can't go one more step, when our hearts feel heavy, when our minds become dull, when our spirits are burned out, we have the *parakletos*, who comes alongside us, puts His everlasting arms around us, and gently walks with us to the finish.

—ANNE GRAHAM LOTZ
Just Give Me Jesus

What part of your life do you need to surrender and entrust to the Lord?

_____

_____

_____

_____

_____

_____

_____

_____

_____

_____

_____

_____

_____

September

*The brightest gem in the crown
of God is His goodness.*
CHARLES SPURGEON

September 1

God is faithful; he will not let you
be tempted beyond what you can bear.
1 CORINTHIANS 10:13 NIV

God came down and lived in this same world as a man. He showed us how to live in this world, subject to its vicissitudes and necessities, that we might be changed—not into an angel or a storybook princess, not wafted into another world, but changed into saints in this world. The secret is Christ in me, not me in a different set of circumstances.

—ELISABETH ELLIOT
Keep a Quiet Heart

What method do you use to resist temptation?

_____

_____

_____

_____

_____

_____

_____

_____

_____

_____

_____

_____

September 2

If someone says, "I love God" and hates his brother, he is a liar.
1 JOHN 4:20

Don't you just hate hypocrisy in the church? For many of you it's a major reason why you don't come to church. In the movie *The Apostle*, starring Robert Duvall, we see a preacher who gets in trouble. He even kills a man, but he runs to a new town and continues to preach.

Certainly, over the last 30 years, Hollywood has done a number on preachers and priests. And time after time they are painted in a very unflattering way, usually as hypocrites or a bunch of out-of-touch airheads, or mean, cruel sickos. If you combine all of that with the charlatan TV evangelists, well, it's not a pretty picture.

But the truth is, all of us preachers struggle with hypocrisy and not always practicing what we preach. I sure do. But I have good news. I've only known one preacher in my life who had no trace of hypocrisy. And He's alive today—His name is Jesus. All the rest of us fall short, but Jesus never does. So put your focus and your faith in Him.

—BRYANT WRIGHT
Right from the Heart

Is there any hypocrisy in your life? Write out a prayer asking God to help you "practice what you preach" or live your life more like Jesus every day.

_____

_____

_____

_____

_____

September 3

I know that this will turn out for my deliverance
through your prayer and the supply of the Spirit of Jesus Christ.
PHILIPPIANS 1:19

Why was Paul convinced of his deliverance? His statement, "I know that this will turn out for my deliverance" is a quote of the Greek version of Job 13:16.

Paul knew he could trust God to deliver him just as God had delivered Job. He was confident his circumstances would work out for good, whether he was released from prison, vindicated at his trial, and delivered from execution, or passed into glory as a martyr. You may not face the same trials as Paul, but whatever your circumstances, the same confident trust is available to you.

—JOHN MACARTHUR
Truth for Today

Is there a situation you aren't trusting God to deliver you through? Confess it now and pray for a spirit of confidence and thanksgiving, no matter how He chooses to work things out.

_____

_____

_____

_____

_____

_____

_____

_____

September 4

May the God of peace Himself sanctify
you completely; and may your whole spirit, soul,
and body be preserved blameless.
1 THESSALONIANS 5:23

If we always feel good and look good and lead a good life; if our kids always behave and our home is always orderly and our bank account is always sufficient and we are patient and kind and thoughtful, others shrug because they're capable of that, too.

On the other hand, if we have a splitting headache, the kids are screaming, the phone is ringing, the supper is burning yet we are still patient, kind, and thoughtful, the world sits up and takes notice. The world knows that kind of behavior is not natural. It's supernatural.

—ANNE GRAHAM LOTZ
Just Give Me Jesus

What kind of behavior will make you blameless before God?

September 5

*Having been justified by faith, we have peace
with God through our Lord Jesus Christ.*
ROMANS 5:1

A part from God there is no lasting quenching of our spiritual hunger and thirst.

Each of us was created in the image and likeness of God. We were made for God's fellowship, and our hearts can never be satisfied without His communion. Just as iron is attracted to a magnet, the soul in its state of hunger is drawn to God.

—BILLY GRAHAM
The Secret of Happiness

What does it mean to have peace with God?

_____

_____

_____

_____

_____

_____

_____

_____

_____

_____

_____

_____

September 6

Whatever things you ask
when you pray, believe that you receive them,
and you will have them.

MARK 11:24

With God, there is only the infinite NOW. Therefore, by faith we must grasp the fact that all the blessings we shall ever need are already deposited in the Treasury of Heaven.

Money in any checking account will stay right there until the owner cashes a check in the present. Even so, we shall receive God's blessings only as we claim them one by one in the present. Faith in the future tense is hope—not faith.

A sure sign that our hope has passed into faith is when we stop begging God and begin thanking Him for the answer to our prayer.

—CATHERINE MARSHALL
Moments that Matter

Does God wish to give you everything you ask for in prayer?

_____

_____

_____

_____

_____

_____

_____

_____

September 7

Be strong and of good courage; do not be afraid, nor be dismayed,
for the LORD your God is with you wherever you go.
JOSHUA 1:9

Maybe because I'm the baby of the family, I like being "accompanied." Whether it's vacation or a trip to the store, you'll hear me say, "Want to come?" I drag people everywhere.

It's great comfort that God is with me wherever I go. His purpose is to stick with me. And mine, to stick with Him. I'm never alone. Sometimes I have to let His Word sink deeply into the recesses of my mind in order to remember, "Lord, thank You that Your Word says You will never leave me or forsake me. Even if I feel forsaken. You are here."

I meditate on verses like that night and day. When I do, I enter into God's perfect plan for my life—His purpose—which is for me to walk with Him, think like He thinks, do what He would do. He accompanies me through life.

—MARY GRAHAM
Women of Faith Devotional Bible

Write Hebrews 13:5 below and commit to memorizing it.

_____

_____

_____

_____

_____

_____

_____

September 8

If we live, we live for the Lord; and if we die,
we die for the Lord. Whether
therefore we live or die, we belong to the Lord.
ROMANS 14:7–9 NEB

The life and death of all of us is in the same Hands. We are always surrounded by the Unseen, among whom are the angels, ministers of fire, explicitly commissioned to guard us. He who keeps us neither slumbers nor sleeps. His love is always awake, always aware, always surrounding and upholding and protecting. If a spear or a bullet finds its target in the flesh of one of His servants, it is not because of inattention on His part. It is because of love.

—ELISABETH ELLIOT
Keep a Quiet Heart

What does it mean to you that we live and die to the Lord?

_____

_____

_____

_____

_____

_____

_____

_____

_____

_____

September 9

Whoever believes in the Son has eternal life.
JOHN 3:36 NRSV

How long is forever? It's a question without an answer that can be humanly comprehended. But, God says that's how long your life will be when you belong to Him. Your life here on Earth is just the beginning, just the childhood of your eternal existence.

Keeping that fact in mind will make a difference in how you choose to live today. It can help balance your priorities as you consider what will last and what will not. It can alleviate your worries about getting older, because there is a new body waiting for you that will never wear out. It can lighten your heart, because there's a time ahead when tears will be a thing of the past.

God's Daily Answer

How does the fact that death isn't truly death, but just a breath away from new life, affect your outlook on your life as you live it in the present?

September 10

For Sadducees say that there is no resurrection—and no angel or spirit; but the Pharisees confess both.
ACTS 23:8

People are so fascinated with the supernatural that Hollywood has produced many blockbuster movies on the supernatural. Yet God's Word is still the most powerful supernatural book in print. The supernatural power of God spoke the creative word and the sun, the moon, and the stars leapt into being. A supernatural God divided the Red Sea (Exodus 14:21), shut the lions' mouths for Daniel (Daniel 6:22) and sent His Son in the world to be born of a virgin. Jesus Christ lived supernaturally. He cast out demons, healed the sick, raised the dead, and commanded nature to obey. He was crucified and died, then rose from His grave. He is coming again in glory called the Rapture—which will be a supernatural event!

The supernatural power of His life and gospel can shatter the shackles of sin and transform you into a child of God. If you want a supernatural change, Jesus never fails.

—JOHN HAGEE
Life Lessons to Live By

Do you believe that the supernatural power of God presented in the Bible is still available to you today?

September 11

The LORD does not see as man sees;
for man looks at the outward appearance,
but the LORD looks at the heart.
1 SAMUEL 16:7

How wonderful that God calls the seemingly unqualified to serve Him. Few of us are the eldest, the brightest, the most beautiful, or the most gifted. But God does not judge us by our outward appearance. . . .

God is not distracted by style, personality, appearance, or achievement. His gaze pierces the flesh and weighs the heart. Then He places His hand upon sincere souls and turns shepherds into kings.

—ALICIA BRITT CHOLE
Pure Joy

How much time do you spend developing your spiritual heart?

_____

_____

_____

_____

_____

_____

_____

_____

_____

_____

_____

September 12

Does not the potter have power over the clay?
ROMANS 9:21

Jesus makes suffering understandable: as the Potter, He uses suffering as the pressure on the wet "clay" of our lives. Under His gentle, loving touch, our lives are molded into a "shape" that pleases Him. But the shape that is so skillfully wrought is not enough. He not only desires our lives to be useful, He also wants our character to be radiant. And so He places us in the furnace of affliction until our "colors" are revealed—colors that reflect the beauty of His own character.

—ANNE GRAHAM LOTZ
Just Give Me Jesus

If you were a piece of clay in the Potter's hands, what kind of a vessel would He create?

September 13

But now in Christ Jesus you who once were far off have been brought near by the blood of Christ. For He Himself is our peace, who has made both one, and has broken down the middle wall of separation.
EPHESIANS 2:13–14

When the charter of the United Nations was signed in October 1945, its stated purposes were to maintain peace and security, solve problems, and promote harmony among nations. Since 1945, however, there have been only twenty-six days when there was not an armed conflict somewhere in the world. But let's not blame nations alone. How many days have you gone without a conflict of some sort—large or small—between you and another person? Given the human propensity for conflict, it's no wonder the Old Testament prophets looked forward to the coming of the Prince of Peace. We're all thirsty for the lasting world peace we don't experience here on earth. But with God's help, we can find personal peace and in turn become peacemakers in the world around us.

—DAVID JEREMIAH
1 Minute a Day

What does peace mean to you? Do you think that we will ever have world peace before Christ's return? If not, does that mean we shouldn't strive to be peacemakers in the world around us?

September 14

Whatever things are true, whatever things are noble, whatever things are just, whatever things are pure, whatever things are lovely, . . . if there is any virtue and if there is anything praiseworthy—meditate on these things.
PHILIPPIANS 4:8

Have you ever had someone say, "You need to change your attitude"? How we approach the challenges of life determines the kind of person we become. If we ponder negative things, our frame of mind will soon turn sour, pessimistic, and negative. If we fill our minds with the things of God, however, the opposite will occur, and we will begin to see the world as God sees it. God wants us to be transformed into people who love to please Him through willing obedience. That transformation begins in the mind and transcends into an attitude of gratitude.

—JACK COUNTRYMAN
Time with God for Fathers

What are some true, noble, just, pure, and lovely things to think on? Write them down and do what God's Word says—"meditate on these things."

September 15

He is a shield to those who walk in integrity.
PROVERBS 2:7 NASB

In the movie *Liar, Liar*, Jim Carey starred as the profane attorney who was incapable of lying for an entire day after his son makes a birthday wish that his dad would stop lying.

Lying has become a pervasive problem. Have you fallen into the habit?

It seems that today's "me first" mindset places very little value on honesty and personal integrity. Truth is sacrificed on the altar of self-advancement. At the time, you may think that lying will make your life easier, but one lie almost always requires another and another and another. You have to remember everything you said to keep from confusing your lies.

But when you tell the truth, you don't have to remember what you said. That makes life a lot less complicated!

—BRYANT WRIGHT
Right from the Heart

Which life have you created for yourself?

_____

_____

_____

_____

_____

_____

_____

_____

September 16

Blessed are the poor in spirit,
For theirs is the kingdom of heaven.
MATTHEW 5:3

Happy are the meek. Happy are the yielded. Happy are those who trustingly put their lives, their fortunes, and their futures in the capable hands of their Creator. Happy are those who "let go and let God."

—BILLY GRAHAM
The Secret of Happiness

Have you ever considered letting God renew your life every day?

September 17

This is the day the LORD has made;
We will rejoice and be glad in it.
PSALM 118:24

As we open our eyes each morning, God sets before us a priceless present. Unique, fresh, and full of potential, each day God gives us *time*.

"Rejoice!" the psalmist says. Has God granted you another day? "Rejoice and be glad in it!" . . .

With each new day, God gives us time as a gracious gift. Rejoice!

—ALICIA BRITT CHOLE
Pure Joy

When was the last time you thanked God for giving you one more day?

September 18

Be merciful, just as your Father also is merciful.
LUKE 6:36

To be kind toward others is merely doing to them what we would like them to do to us. This kindness is linked to mercy. God's love is manifested by and through His mercy. Mercy is an act of kindness. It is also an expression of tenderness.

—R. C. SPROUL
Loved by God

If mercy is an act of kindness, does your daily life reflect kindness to others?

September 19

Therefore humble yourselves under the mighty hand of
God, that He may exalt you in due time.
1 PETER 5:6

Are you anxious for God to work out His plan for your life? As believers, we all want God to do great things for us and through us, and we want Him to do those things now! But sometimes God's timetable does not coincide with our own. It's worth noting, however, that God's timetable is always perfect.

The next time you find your patience tested to the limit, remember that the world unfolds according to God's plan, not ours. Sometimes we must wait patiently, and that's as it should be. After all, think how patient God has been with us.

—CRISWELL FREEMAN
Purpose for Everyday Living

Think back to a time when God seemed to take too long to work in your life. In what
ways are you now thankful for His perfect timing?

September 20

And of the angels He says:
"Who makes His angels spirits
And His ministers a flame of fire."
HEBREWS 1:7

Did you know that you are being watched all the time by angels? "For we have been made a spectacle to the world, both to angels and to men" (1 Corinthians 4:9). The word *spectacle* comes from first-century arenas where sports fans went to watch talented athletes. To be "made a spectacle" means to be made an intense visual observation.

"Therefore we also, since we are surrounded by so great a cloud of witnesses, let us lay aside every weight, and the sin which so easily ensnares us" (Hebrews 12:1). Those "witnesses" are the angels in heaven, and the righteous who have died, watching you. In 1 Timothy 5:21, Paul makes it clear that you need to be careful what you say and what you do because the angels of God are watching.

—JOHN HAGEE
Life Lessons to Live By

Have you ever thought the angels in heaven are watching what you say and do every day? How important are the words you speak and the impressions you give to others?

_____

_____

_____

_____

_____

_____

September 21

Therefore if anyone is in Christ, he is a new creature; the old things have passed away; behold, new things have come!

2 CORINTHIANS 5:17 NASB

So what is so special about a new year? Once this calendar year expires, there will never be another one. Days, months, seasons, and holidays will all eventually return, but once this year is over, it's over.

Maybe that is why we tend to schedule our resolutions for change at the beginning of each New Year, hoping the old habits won't return, much as that particular year won't return. But real change requires so much more than a New Year's resolution. It's tough to break established habits. But remember that there is hope for the person who sincerely desires change. The power for real change means admitting that we are helpless to do it on our own. Lasting change requires the help of the Lord. Why don't you ask *His* help?

—BRYANT WRIGHT
Right from the Heart

What old habits do you need to change to become the new creature in Christ that God wants you to be?

September 22

Do you want to be truly rich?
You already are if you are happy and good.
1 TIMOTHY 6:6 TLB

Many people seem to be pursuing great wealth these days. Maybe you are one of those people. Do you believe that riches can bring you security and happiness? Do you have a deep desire to lead a glamorous lifestyle? If so, you are apt to find, as so many others have before you, that wealth cannot help you become the person God created you to be. But contentment can.

Being content with what God has given you, allows you to look past the distractions and attachments of wealth and possessions and focus on those things—love, faith, hope, godliness—that will bring you security and happiness both in this life and the life to come.

God's Daily Answer

Are you able to find security and contentment in God alone, or do you also rely on your material wealth?

September 23

Now therefore,
Arise, O LORD God, to Your resting place,
You and the ark of Your strength.
Let Your priests, O LORD God, be clothed with salvation,
And let Your saints rejoice in goodness.
2 CHRONICLES 6:41

The spiritual warfare that Satan wages for your soul begins in your mind. Thus Paul says that we are to "take the helmet of salvation" (Ephesians 6:17), for the helmet protects the head.

You are wounded in your head when you are controlled by conditions such as depression, anger, and fear. You are wounded in your head when your thoughts are negative and suspicious and your imaginations are vulgar and sensual. When you find yourself thinking about something that is not of God, put on the helmet of your salvation in Christ, which brings renewal and wholeness. . . . If Christ is in you, you always have the hope that overcomes the enemy!

—JOHN HAGEE
Life Lessons to Live By

What is your greatest challenge today? How often do you come to the Lord in prayer when trouble walks into your life?

_____

_____

_____

_____

_____

September 24

The secret of the Lᴏʀᴅ is with those who fear Him,
And He will show them His covenant.

PSALM 25:14

When we need help, we wish we knew somebody who is wise enough to tell us what to do, reachable when we need him, and even able to help us. God is. Omniscient, omnipresent, omnipotent—everything we need. The issue is confidence in the Shepherd Himself, a confidence so complete that we offer ourselves without any reservation whatsoever and determine to do what He says.

—ELISABETH ELLIOT
Keep a Quiet Heart

When you need help, whom do you run to and why?

September 25

And hope does not disappoint us, because God has poured out his love into our hearts by the Holy Spirit, whom he has given us.
ROMANS 5:5 NIV

You may not know what your tomorrows hold, but as a believer in Christ Jesus, you know the One who does. And He has a perfect plan for your life. He doesn't want you to waste precious time today worrying about to-morrow . . . about things you have no control over or situations that will never come to pass. Instead Jesus wants you to trust Him and to give Him thanks today for what He has blessed you with presently, as well as for what He has in store for you tomorrow. Yes. Sight unseen. That kind of thanksgiving is called faith.

The Lord has given you very great and wonderful promises concerning your future. He assures you that His plan for you is to bless you and not to harm you. Life will not be pain-free, but it will be perfect for who you are and for where God wants to take you. And as you walk with Him, He will faithfully reveal His plan to you one step at a time.

—KARLA DORNACHER
Give Thanks

Is it difficult for you to trust God and to give control of your future to Him?

September 26

But without faith it is impossible to please Him, for he who comes to God must believe that He is, and that He is a rewarder of those who diligently seek Him.

HEBREWS 11:6

The beautiful thing about faith is that it declares our weakness, while at the same time it proclaims the strength and trustworthiness of God and His complete and willing ability to do what we cannot. A lack of faith insults God, even as it puts foolish confidence in our own abilities. Faith is not wishful thinking or believing what we know isn't true; it is the conviction that God will always do what He promises to do, regardless of the circumstances we are facing in life.

—JACK COUNTRYMAN
Time with God for Fathers

What do you think about a lack of faith being an insult to God?

September 27

The righteousness of Your testimonies is everlasting;
Give me understanding, and I shall live.
PSALM 119:144

Nothing can take the place of a daily devotional life with Christ. The great missionary Hudson Taylor said, "Never mind how great the pressure is—only where the pressure lies. Never let it come between you and the Lord, then the greater pressure, the more it presses you to His heart!" Our quiet time, our prayer time, the time we spend in the Word is absolutely essential for a happy Christian life.

—BILLY GRAHAM
The Secret of Happiness

What do you think is meant by the word "everlasting"?

September 28

Not everyone who says to Me, "Lord, Lord," shall enter the kingdom of heaven, but he who does the will of My Father in heaven.
MATTHEW 7:21

In describing one's beliefs, actions are far better descriptors than words. Yet far too many of us spend more energy talking about our beliefs than living by them—with predictable consequences. Today and every day, make certain that your actions are guided by God's Word and by the conscience that He has placed in your heart. Don't treat your faith as if it were separate from your everyday life. Weave your beliefs into the very fabric of your day. When you do, God will honor your good works, and your good works will honor God.

—CRISWELL FREEMAN
Purpose for Everyday Living

Is your life a picture book of your creed? Are your actions congruent with your beliefs?

September 29

But You, O Lord, do not be far from Me;
O My Strength, hasten to help Me!
PSALM 22:19

In Psalm 22 David boldly complained that God was not hearing his prayers: "My God, My God, why have You forsaken Me?" He told God—as if the Lord didn't already know—that "trouble is near . . . You have brought Me to the dust of death." As his enemies surrounded him, the situation looked grim for David.

Maybe your situation doesn't look good right now. In times of crisis, however, what others are attempting is not as important as what God is doing. The advance of the enemy, their weapons, their proximity—none of these is as important as God's presence and activity. When we focus on God in even the worst of predicaments, we always discover that He is near, and that His presence is our deliverance.

—HENRY AND RICHARD BLACKABY
Discovering God's Daily Agenda

What is a difficult situation you're facing where God doesn't seem near? Write a prayer below focusing on the promise of God's presence and deliverance from your circumstances.

_____

_____

_____

_____

_____

_____

September 30

Then the LORD said to Moses, "Behold, I will rain bread from heaven for you. And the people shall go out and gather a certain quota every day, that I may test them, whether they will walk in My law or not."
EXODUS 16:4

God started teaching humanity about His provision for our lives through the manna that fell from heaven every morning after the children of Israel escaped from Egypt and were on their way to the Promised Land. That it was God's miraculous provision was undeniable, and it was as regular as the rising of the sun. But if you were an Israelite, you still had "to mind your own business, and to work with your own hands" (1 Thessalonians 4:11). The message is clear. You should pray as though everything depends on God, and you should work as though everything depends on you, and good things will happen. God is with you, the Holy Spirit is in you, and the anointing of heaven is upon you. Put your hand in the hand of God.

—JOHN HAGEE
Life Lessons to Live By

God has promised to bless and provide for His children, but do you sometimes see His blessings (a home, family, clothes, food) as something that you have provided yourself?

October

*Faith expects from God
what is beyond all expectation.*
ANDREW MURRAY

October 1

*All things work together for good
to those who love God, to those who are the
called according to His purpose.*
ROMANS 8:28

As long as we maintain our dependence on God, He is able to take all the evils that befall us and weave them into His master plan. Our omnipotent God can make even "the wrath of man to praise Him." He can take any sins, any evil, any calamity—no matter where it originated—and make it "work together for good to those who love God."

—CATHERINE MARSHALL
Moments that Matter

Have you discovered your purpose? If so, what is it?

_____

_____

_____

_____

_____

_____

_____

_____

_____

_____

_____

October 2

We walk by faith, not by sight.
2 CORINTHIANS 5:7

The walk of becoming more like Christ takes place when we live by faith. When we judge everything by what we see, however, we will have difficulty growing.

Remember the twelve spies Israel sent into Canaan (Numbers 13)? Ten came back and said they felt like grasshoppers in a land of giants. Those ten walked by sight. But Joshua and Caleb had faith, knowing that God was on their side. Ten didn't think God could handle the circumstances, but two knew He is bigger than any situation.

—JOHN MACARTHUR
Truth for Today

In what ways are you living by faith? living by sight? Write a prayer confessing your sight (unbelief), and ask the King of kings to increase your faith and spiritual growth in Him.

October 3

Not forsaking our own assembling together, as is the habit of some, but encouraging one another; and all the more as you see the day drawing near.
HEBREWS10:25 NASB

Have you ever thought of the similarities of the local church and the neighborhood bar? In both places:

People come looking for fellowship.

People want to go where they are accepted.

People want to go where their spirits will be lifted.

People go where they like the music.

Like a priest, the bartender serves by listening to people's troubles. But the differences are profound: the bar is centered on booze and the church is centered on Jesus Christ. The bar offers a way to escape problems. The church offers a way to face them, get through them, and overcome them.

The spirit inside the bar lowers one's guard when it comes to temptation and sin. The spirit of the true church encourages people to turn from sin and turn to God.

In short, the neighborhood bar may be a substitute for the environment of the church, but it never comes close to providing the meaning and purpose found in a Christ-centered church.

—BRYANT WRIGHT
Right from the Heart

What are other ways we try to escape problems instead of facing and overcoming them?

October 4

"Now therefore," says the LORD,
"Turn to me with all your heart,
With fasting, with weeping, and with mourning." . . .
Then the LORD will be zealous for His land,
And pity His people.
JOEL 2:12, 18

True repentance is not a pleasant experience. It involves a broken heart and deep sorrow. But whenever we are brokenhearted and genuinely humbled by the reality of our sin, God will have compassion on us and forgive our sin.

Sometimes in our pride, though, we think that not even God can forgive us. Know that such thoughts are the enemy's lies, and counter them with the truth of Scripture. The truth of 1 John 1:8–9 is a powerful weapon when Satan whispers in your ear that you've committed the unforgivable.

—HENRY AND RICHARD BLACKABY
Discovering God's Daily Agenda

Is there a sin you're holding onto which you don't think God can or will forgive?
Write 1 John 1:8–9. Pray a prayer of repentance now and recite this verse, claiming
His promise to forgive you and cleanse you from all unrighteousness.

October 5

If you love Me, keep My commandments.
JOHN 14:15

The cross is not just a symbol of love or a fashion statement. The cross is your daily decision to deny yourself, your rights, your wants, your dreams, your plans, your goals, and deliberately, wholeheartedly, unreservedly live out your commitment to God's will and God's way and God's Word and God's wisdom. The cross is your decision to live for Him. Period.

—ANNE GRAHAM LOTZ
Just Give Me Jesus

Who is your first love?

October 6

I, the LORD, search the heart,
I test the mind,
Even to give every man according to his ways,
According to the fruit of his doings.
JEREMIAH 17:10

It's an old saying and a true one: First, you make your habits, and then your habits make you. Some habits will inevitably bring you closer to God; other habits will lead you away from the path He has chosen for you. If you sincerely desire to improve your spiritual health, you must honestly examine the habits that make up the fabric of your day. And you must abandon those habits that are displeasing to God.

If you trust God, and if you keep asking for His help, He can transform your life. If at first you don't succeed, keep praying. God is listening, and He's ready to help you become a better person if you ask Him.

—CRISWELL FREEMAN
Purpose for Everyday Living

What habits do you need to ask God to help you change? Will you ask Him today?

October 7

If we confess our sins, He is faithful and just to forgive us our sins and to cleanse us from all unrighteousness.

1 JOHN 1:9

Sometimes I shudder just thinking about it—that feeling of being ashamed. The dictionary says *shame* is a "painful emotion caused by consciousness of guilt, shortcoming, or impropriety."* And it is painful, especially the shame that comes after we've done something we know we shouldn't have. Some people avoid the pain of shame by suppressing their sense of right and wrong, by ignoring their conscience. Instead, why not let shame be a teacher that leads us to God and His forgiveness? The pain of shame can do something else: it can motivate us to avoid experiencing that same pain again in the future. No one enjoys the feeling of shame, but put it to work for you. Let it drive you into God's loving arms of forgiveness, and let the memory of it keep you on the right path.

—DAVID JEREMIAH
1 Minute a Day

Have you ever been weighed down by the crushing burden of shame and guilt? Do you ever feel like you need to be washed clean? How does it make you feel when God promises to lift you up, forgive you, and cleanse you from all unrighteousness?

---

* *Merriam-Webster's Collegiate Dictionary*, 11th ed. (Springfield, MA: Merriam-Webster, Inc., 2007), 1143.

294

October 8

He who loves me will be loved
by My Father, and I will love him.
JOHN 14:21

Jesus purposefully pursued quiet time with His Father—a sacred space worthy of sacrifice, where the urgent bows to the eternal; a gift—not a waste—of time for God.

Carving out moments to be alone with God is an exercise in stillness where we elevate Creator above creation, "being" above "doing." Where we listen to the One who is always listening to us.

Resting in God's presence, our soul enjoys a banquet from God's Word. Our minds forge an alliance with truth, and dreams are born.

—ALICIA BRITT CHOLE
Pure Joy

How much time do you spend alone with God? Explain.

_____

_____

_____

_____

_____

_____

_____

_____

_____

_____

October 9

Concerning this [thorn in the flesh] I pleaded with the Lord three times that it might depart from me. And He said to me, "My grace is sufficient for you, for My strength is made perfect in weakness." Therefore most gladly I will rather boast in my infirmities, that the power of Christ may rest upon me.

2 CORINTHIANS 12:8–9

The power of sin and the presence of evil in this world are both very real—but neither one is any match for the love of God. After all, God is in the redemption business, and Jesus has said that his grace will be enough for whatever we face. There is nothing you or I will face today, tomorrow, or ever that we will face alone. Jesus will be there with us, and he will provide everything we need to walk through it.

—SHEILA WALSH
Good Morning, Lord

It's a promise: God's grace will be enough whatever circumstances we face. When has his grace clearly been instrumental in helping you deal with temptation, evil, loss, or pain?

October 10

Then He took the five loaves and the two fish,
And looking up to heaven, He blessed and broke them,
And gave them to the disciples to set before the multitude.
LUKE 9:16

How many times have we said to God, "I need a miracle"? A child is sick, a bill can't be paid, a job is lost, or any number of things can happen to make life seem impossible. Jesus demonstrated to His disciples and to the multitude who needed something to eat that through Him all things are possible. When life throws you a curve, run to God. His Spirit is willing, and your miracle may be just around the corner.

—JACK COUNTRYMAN
Time with God for Mothers

Do you run to God when faced with the impossible, or do you lean on your own understanding of the situation to get you through it?

October 11

You shall love the Lord your God with all your heart,
with all your soul, and with all your strength.
DEUTERONOMY 6:5

What is it that God really wants from us? God summarized His law in a single verse: each of us is to love God with all our heart, all our soul, and all our might.

God wants far more than external conformity to His laws. He seeks enthusiastic obedience as a response of love for Him, not obedience stemming from a sense of duty or obligation.

So, as God's child, flee from anything that draws you away from loving your heavenly Father. Realize that a love relationship with God truly is His desire for your life. Obedience to His law is simply a gauge of your love; obedience is not God's ultimate goal for you—He wants your heart.

—HENRY AND RICHARD BLACKABY
Discovering God's Daily Agenda

Is there any activity in your life that draws you away from completely loving your
Father? or any part of your heart you have not given to Him?

October 12

Blessed are the pure in heart,
for they shall see God.
MATTHEW 5:8

Jesus said, "Happy are the pure in heart." Now, we should be able to take that for just what it means. If the heart is the seat of affection, then our love toward God must be pure. If the heart is the center of our motives, then our motives must be pure. If the heart is the residence of our wills, then our wills must be yielded to Christ. We are to be pure in love, pure in motive, and pure in desire.

—BILLY GRAHAM
The Secret of Happiness

What does it take for someone to be pure in heart?

October 13

Some people are like land that gets plenty of rain. The land produces a good crop for those who work it, and it receives God's blessings.
HEBREWS 6:7 NCV

Have you ever wished you could multiply your money? Well, I have wonderful news for you: God is able to do it. Of course, that shouldn't come as a surprise to us. He multiplied oil and meal for a poor widow and her son (1 Kings 17:14). He multiplied the strength of outnumbered Israelite soldiers in battle after battle (Judges 7). And He multiplied fish and loaves on a couple of Galilean hillsides. Clearly, God is a Master of multiplication.

But we must be obedient to God's instruction for His principle of multiplication to set into action. This is especially hard when we can't figure out in advance how God is going to provide for our needs.

—ROBERT MORRIS
The Blessed Life

What situation in your life are you facing right now that you can't see how God is going to provide? What can you do to help yourself stand strong in your faith and believe that He will do as He's promised?

October 14

*"They shall be Mine," says the L*ORD *of hosts,*
"On the day that I make them My jewels.
And I will spare them
As a man spares his own son who serves him."
MALACHI 3:17

We are God's treasures, and He has declared that we are His jewels. Often we may not realize that to God we are more precious than diamonds, rubies, or gold. Each one of God's children is a treasure that is more meaningful to Him than anything we could ever imagine. Therefore, let each day be filled with His love as we receive the blessing God so generously wishes to give.

—JACK COUNTRYMAN
Time with God for Mothers

Do you value yourself and others the same way God values us?

_____

_____

_____

_____

_____

_____

_____

_____

_____

_____

October 15

*Be steadfast, immovable, always abounding
in the work of the Lord, knowing that your labor
is not in vain in the Lord.*

1 CORINTHIANS 15:58

One day, God Himself will take your face in His hands and gently wipe away your tears as He reassures you there will be no more suffering. There will be no more broken homes or broken hearts, broken lives or broken dreams. You can look forward with hope, because one day there will be no more separation, no more scars, and no more suffering in My Father's House. It's the home of your dreams!

—ANNE GRAHAM LOTZ
Heaven: My Father's House

Describe what this verse means to you and your daily life.

_____

_____

_____

_____

_____

_____

_____

_____

_____

_____

_____

October 16

Many waters cannot quench love,
Nor can the floods drown it.
If a man would give for love
All the wealth of his house,
It would be utterly despised.
SONG OF SONGS 8:7

My Love for you is unquenchable. It is even stronger than the bond between a mother and her baby. *Though she may forget the baby at her breast, I will not forget you!* You are so precious to Me that *I have engraved you on the palms of both My hands.* So, forgetting you is out of the question. Not only do I remember you constantly, I also have compassion on you continually.

I want you to *really come to know—practically, through experience—My Love, which far surpasses mere knowledge.* The Holy Spirit, who lives in your innermost being, will help in this amorous quest. Ask Him to fill you up completely with My fullness so that you may have *the richest measure of the divine Presence:* becoming *a body wholly filled and flooded* with Me! Thus you can experience My Love in full measure.

—SARAH YOUNG
Jesus Lives

What is the greatest act of love you've ever witnessed? How did it affect you? Now consider how much greater is Jesus' Love for you! How can you respond to this awesome Love?

October 17

If the Lord delights in us, then He will bring us into this land
and give it to us, "a land which flows with milk and honey."
NUMBERS 14:8

R emember that God's provision for the needs of your life is backed by
His promise. David said, "I have been young, and now am old; yet I have
not seen the righteous forsaken, nor his descendants begging bread" (Psalm
37:25). God's provision is for all your needs—your salvation, finances,
home, healing from diseases, and deliverance from every form of addiction.
Let faith explode in your soul. God wants to give these to you more than you
want to receive them.

—JOHN HAGEE
Life Lessons to Live By

How does it make you feel to know that God's desire to bless you is greater than your
desire to be blessed?

October 18

We are in Him who is true,
in His Son Jesus Christ.
1 JOHN 5:20

We have been shown the way of acceptance on every page of the life of Jesus. It sprang from love and from trust. He set His face like a flint toward Jerusalem. He took up the Cross of His own will. No one could take His life from Him. He deliberately laid it down. He calls us to take up our crosses. That is a different thing from capitulation or resignation. It is a glad and voluntary YES.

—ELISABETH ELLIOT
Keep a Quiet Heart

How well acquainted are you with Jesus Christ?

October 19

Your righteousness is an everlasting righteousness,
And Your law is truth.
PSALM 119:142

Each of us must become as a little child and by faith grasp what we cannot altogether understand. But faith is not a blind leap in the dark! It is instead based squarely on what God has done for us in Jesus Christ. Our faith has a firm foundation, because it is not based on speculation or wishful thinking, but upon God and His Word. God can be trusted to keep His promises to us.

—BILLY GRAHAM
The Secret of Happiness

What must you change to be in right standing with God?

October 20

In Your presence is fullness of joy.
PSALM 16:11

David didn't have an easy life either before or after he became king. He was familiar with false accusation, homelessness, failure, betrayal, and family strife. Yet his psalms are filled with expressions of joy.

In spite of circumstances, David chose joy. He could have chosen pity, anger, loneliness, frustration, or fear. He chose joy.

—ALICIA BRITT CHOLE
Pure Joy

How much time do you spend in God's presence?

October 21

He will speak peace
To His people and to His saints.
PSALM 85:8

If God says, "I forgive you," who are you to say, "Thank You, God, but I can't forgive myself"? Are your standards higher than His? Are you more righteous than He is? If God says, "I forgive you," then the only appropriate response is to say, "God, thank You. I don't deserve it, but I accept it. And to express my gratitude, I, in turn, forgive that person who has sinned against me."

—ANNE GRAHAM LOTZ
Just Give Me Jesus

When did you make peace with God? Describe that experience.

_____

_____

_____

_____

_____

_____

_____

_____

_____

_____

_____

October 22

I can do all things through Christ who strengthens me.
PHILIPPIANS 4:13

Are you willing to dream big dreams? Hopefully so; after all, God promises that we can do "all things" through Him. Yet most of us . . . live far below our potential. We take half measures; we dream small dreams; we waste precious time and energy on the distractions of the world. But God has other plans for us. Our Creator intends that we live faithfully, hopefully, courageously, and abundantly. He knows that we are capable of so much more; and He wants us to do the things we're capable of doing; and He wants us to start doing those things now.

—CRISWELL FREEMAN
Purpose for Everyday Living

In what way are you not living up to your fullest potential? Pray and ask God to help you change so that you can live to the level of abundance He wants for you.

October 23

Wash me thoroughly from my iniquity,
And cleanse me from my sin.
PSALMS 51:2 NASB

A re you riddled with guilt?

You need to be free from guilt, for it saps you physically, emotionally, and spiritually. When it comes to guilt, the best way to avoid it is simply to do what is right.

When you don't, you first need to confess your sin to God with a genuine desire to get things right. I promise that when you pursue the forgiveness of God through Jesus Christ, with an attitude of seeking to get things right it will free you of guilt. He wipes the slate clean.

Second, seek forgiveness from those that you've wronged. Make restitution.

Third, forgive yourself. Some struggle with this, but you should recognize that when God has forgiven you, you can forgive yourself.

Fourth, don't confuse forgiveness with the removal of consequences. God forgives immediately, but you have to deal with the consequences of your sin.

The good news is you can be free of guilt when you seek to get things right— God's way.

—BRYANT WRIGHT
Right from the Heart

Which of the steps above do you need to apply in your own life?

_____

_____

_____

The Son of Man has come to seek and to save that which was lost.
LUKE 19:10

Hear how Jesus himself once described his life's mission: "The Son of Man came to find and restore the lost" (Luke 19:10 MSG). Jesus didn't come to argue with religious leaders, heal those who were sick, or even paint a more accurate picture of his Father. Jesus came primarily to find and restore every lost human being, a work he ultimately did on the cross. And isn't it interesting that *the lost* can be translated as "broken beyond repair"? Have you ever felt broken to that degree, despairing, afraid you weren't going to make it? I love Luke 19:10 because it says that if we feel that way, we can take heart because that's why Jesus came. And that's love.

—SHEILA WALSH
Good Morning, Lord

In what ways, if any, are you lost now? What does the fact that Jesus loves you mean to you in your current circumstances?

October 25

Let us hold fast the confession of our hope without wavering,
for He who promised is faithful.
HEBREWS 10:23

Your body is an amazing creation. It has the ability to move around, to feel a summer breeze, to hear a crack of thunder, to differentiate between the taste of a strawberry and a kiwi.

Taking care of such an incredible masterpiece is a big responsibility. But, despite its complexity, God has kept the maintenance of your body rather simple. Get enough sleep. Eat a balanced diet. Get up and move around on a regular basis. Praise God when you're feeling well. Ask for His help and healing when you're not.

God's Daily Answer

Your body is a gift from God. Why not take a moment right now and thank Him for the miracle He has entrusted into your care?

October 26

We have a building from God, a house
not made with hands, eternal in the heavens.
2 CORINTHIANS 5:1

Earth's heartaches are healed by the promises of God. When we are home at last, the homesickness will be over. We shall praise the King who knew how to cut eternal doorways in mere holes cut in sod. Joy belongs to all those who understand that earth is but a rehearsal for heaven. On dim evenings, if you squint at sunsets, you can all but see the promise. In our Father's house there really are many mansions—and one of them is ours.

—CALVIN MILLER
Into the Depths of God

Have you ever asked yourself what God has planned for you in heaven?

October 27

For I am the LORD, I do not change.
MALACHI 3:6

To call upon God as "our Father" speaks of a Person who never changes. Why is that important? Because everything in your life is changing. People change, governments change, morals change, society changes, and laws change. You don't think you're changing? Go home and look at an old photo of yourself. You're always changing. Look at a magazine from a few years ago and see how the world has changed. Thank God that He never changes. The Bible says that He is "the Father of lights, with whom there is no variation or shadow of turning" (James 1:17). He is "the same yesterday, today, and forever" (Heb. 13:8). God has no beginning because He always was. He has no ending because He always will be. And He is our Father God.

—JOHN HAGEE
Life Lessons to Live By

Why is an unchanging God important to you?

_____

_____

_____

_____

_____

_____

_____

_____

October 28

Happy are those who think about the poor.
When trouble comes, the LORD will save them.
PSALM 41:1 NCV

Concentration camp survivor Corrie ten Boom correctly observed, "The measure of a life is not its duration but its donation." These words remind us that the quality of our lives is determined not by what we are able to take from others, but instead by what we are able to share with others.

The thread of generosity is woven into the very fabric of Christ's teachings. If we are to be His disciples, then we, too, must be cheerful, generous, courageous givers. Our Savior expects no less from us. And He deserves no less.

—CRISWELL FREEMAN
Purpose for Everyday Living

How will you be a generous giver today?

October 29

Commit your way to the LORD,
Trust also in Him,
And He shall bring it to pass.
PSALM 37:5

A cceptance of discipleship is the utter abandonment of the disciple, the surrender of all rights, to the Master. This abandonment, in all cases, will mean pain. Christ listed some of the troubles His followers could expect, so they would not be taken by surprise and thus discard their faith in Him. He did not offer immunity. He asked for trust.

—ELISABETH ELLIOT
Keep a Quiet Heart

How hard is it for you to trust in the Lord in every area of your life?

_____

_____

_____

_____

_____

_____

_____

_____

_____

_____

_____

_____

October 30

And we know that all things work together for good to those who
love God, to those who are the called according to His purpose.
ROMANS 8:28

On this side of heaven, we will never understand how "all things" can work together for good for God's children. We recognize that not all things in themselves are good, but God knows the ultimate outcome, and we can trust Him in all our circumstances. When facing difficult times, lean on the Lord for strength, courage, and the will to handle the challenges of life. Keep in mind, "If God is for us, who can be against us?" (Romans 8:31). Nothing can ultimately triumph over us, for in the end, God always wins and we win with Him.

—JACK COUNTRYMAN
Time with God for Mothers

Life comes with many ups and downs. Sometimes it seems like there are way more downs than ups. But do you trust that God will ultimately deliver you?

_____

_____

_____

_____

_____

_____

_____

_____

October 31

We all, with unveiled face, beholding as in a mirror the glory
of the Lord, are being transformed into the same image
from glory to glory, just as by the Spirit of the Lord.
2 CORINTHIANS 3:18

As we glorify God, we begin to grow. Because of the great truths revealed in the New Testament, believers can now view God's glory more clearly than those under the law could. As we do, we grow spiritually, moving from one level of glory to the next.

Notice that Paul says the Holy Spirit is the one who energizes our growth. The Holy Spirit infuses our lives with His power, taking us through levels of glory toward the image of Christ.

—JOHN MACARTHUR
Truth for Today

How has your life transformed into the likeness of God?

November

God is never away off somewhere else,
He is always there.
OSWALD CHAMBERS

November 1

As for God, His way is perfect.
PSALM 18:30

Is anyone perfect? No, not anyone on earth. Only God is perfect! And you don't need to be God—not in your own appraisal of yourself or in relation to anybody. You are free to simply be you. There will always be aspects of you that fall short of some idealized goal. As you are able to recognize and accept these aspects, you will have a chance to modify them and improve them. And you will set other people free to do the same.

—NEIL CLARK WARREN
God Said It, Don't Sweat It

What are your spiritual goals to be more like Christ?

_____

_____

_____

_____

_____

_____

_____

_____

_____

_____

_____

November 2

Greater love has no one than this,
than to lay down one's life for his friends.
JOHN 15:13

The only crown Jesus ever wore on earth was a crown of thorns. What does that crown tell us about the love of God the Father? Much every way. For one thing, it tells us that His love is not a sentimental thing, for it was strong enough to hurt His own Son. He could have rescued Him with "legions of angels." He did not do so. What does the crown of thorns tell us about the love of God the Son? It tells us that it was strong enough to deny itself, strong enough to suffer.

—ELISABETH ELLIOT
Keep a Quiet Heart

How much Christian love do you have for your friends?

November 3

*I tell you the truth, unless you change and become like little
children, you will never enter the kingdom of heaven.*
MATTHEW 18:3 NIV

God hears all our prayers, the good and the bad. He is big enough to handle our honest questions, our doubts, and even our anger. God receives our thankful prayers and the not-so-thankful ones, the eloquent ones and the less-than-perfect ones. He accepts our joyful and self-confident prayers as well as our anguished questioning when we experience trauma or loss. I've gone to God when I was afraid, angry, and therefore very honest. It felt good to relate to God in that authentic way—and I could never go back to my old, edited, controlled prayers. Real relationship demands intimate dialogue. Know that God accepts all our prayers because when we pray, we acknowledge our belief that God is in control.

—SHEILA WALSH
Good Morning, Lord

*What interferes with your having that ongoing dialogue with God that you would
like to have?*

November 4

He has made the earth by His power;
He has established the world by His wisdom,
And stretched out the heaven by His understanding.
JEREMIAH 51:15

To pray the words, "Our Father," is a statement of power. Our Father is the Creator of heaven and earth. Isaiah asked, "Who has measured the waters in the hollow of His hand, measured heaven with a span and calculated the dust of the earth in a measure? Weighed the mountains in scales and the hills in a balance?" (Isaiah 40:12). Our Father has. "He counts the number of the stars; He calls them all by name" (Psalm 147:4). Our Father has numbered the hairs on your head (Matthew 10:30), and collected your tears in a bottle (Psalm 56:8). He loves you with an everlasting love. That is powerful.

—JOHN HAGEE
Life Lessons to Live By

Do you sometimes think of God's power in terms of His greatness and His ability to create the heavens and the earth? How does it make you feel to know that that same power is at work in every detail of your life?

November 5

You are my hiding place;
You will protect me from trouble
And surround me with songs of deliverance.
PSALM 32:7 NIV

Throughout life, we must all endure life-changing personal losses that leave us breathless. When we do, God stands ready to protect us. Psalm 147 promises, "He heals the brokenhearted and bandages their wounds" (v. 3 NCV).

When we are troubled, we must call upon God, and, in His own time, and according to His own plan, He *will* heal us. Take your troubles to Him. Seek protection from the One who cannot be moved. The same God who created the universe will protect you if you ask Him . . . so ask Him.

—CRISWELL FREEMAN
Purpose for Everyday Living

What is on your heart that you haven't called upon God for His help?

_____

_____

_____

_____

_____

_____

_____

_____

_____

November 6

Truly our fellowship is with the Father and
with His Son Jesus Christ.

1 JOHN 1:3

Jesus had a humble heart. If He abides in us, pride will never dominate our lives. Jesus had a loving heart. If He dwells within us, hatred and bitterness will never rule us. Jesus had a forgiving and understanding heart. If He lives within us, mercy will temper our relationships with our fellow men.

—BILLY GRAHAM
The Secret of Happiness

How important is fellowship with other believers in your life?

November 7

God is our refuge and strength,
an ever-present help in trouble.
PSALM 46:1 NIV

Though difficulties abound in this world, rejoice that I am always present with you. I can enable you to cope with any and all circumstances, strengthening you as you look trustingly to Me. No matter how hopeless your situation may seem, I assure you that *all things are possible with Me.*

I am the Truth, and therefore I am true to all My promises. They provide a rock-solid foundation on which you can *live and move and have your being.* Since I am the living Word, affirming your trust in My promises is an excellent way to draw near Me. As you bask in the beauty of My Presence, you may find yourself wanting to praise Me. Do not restrain that holy impulse; instead, give it voice. While you are worshiping Me, new hope will grow within you. *Hope in Me, for you will again praise Me for the help of My Presence.*

—SARAH YOUNG
Jesus Lives

Write down the promises of God that mean the most to you. Draw near to Him by affirming your trust in these promises.

November 8

But [a] fruit of the spirit is . . . kindness.
GALATIANS 5:22

A cts of kindness inspire us, whether it's taking time to help an employee at the office, or defending a person who is being picked on by bullies. The recipients of these acts of kindness are always grateful.

The one person who comes to mind when I think of kindness is Jesus Christ. He shows us that God is kind. And because He is so kind to us, we are to be kind to one another.

Especially in a busy world where so many seem to be looking out for number one, acts of kindness are always appreciated.

—BRYANT WRIGHT
Right from the Heart

What acts of kindness can you show today? This week?

November 9

Now abide faith, hope, love, these three;
but the greatest of these is love.
1 CORINTHIANS 13:13

Paul not only distinguishes among faith, hope, and love, but also links them to show that they remain connected and mutually dependent on each other. The biblical concept of hope does not lack the confidence that our cultural concept of hope does.

Rather, hope is faith looking forward to the future. It is a hope that will not disappoint or leave us ashamed.

—R. C. SPROUL
Loved by God

How are faith, hope, and love connected in the life of a Christian?

November 10

The LORD will perfect that which concerns me;
Your mercy, O LORD, endures forever.
PSALM 138:8

To magnify something, you make it look larger, increasing it out of proportion. To talk about ourselves or our activities out of true proportion is dangerous indeed, but when we magnify God, we are on safe ground. We simply cannot say too much about God's goodness or love. The most exaggerated things we can think of will still be far below what is actually the case.

—RICHARD J. FOSTER
Prayer: Finding the Heart's True Home

How would you magnify God today?

November 11

*Count it all joy when you fall
into various trials, knowing that the testing
of your faith produces patience.*
JAMES 1:2–3

Trials, James tells us, prove the authenticity of our faith.
Truth is, we would rather be perfected and completed by viewing a motivational video, attending a challenging conference, reading an inspiring book (about someone else who went through trials), or . . . anything but testing! . . .

We long for controlled, comfortable circumstances. But pure joy is the fruit of tested, patient faith.

—ALICIA BRITT CHOLE
Pure Joy

How do you handle the various trials and testings you face?

_____

_____

_____

_____

_____

_____

_____

_____

_____

_____

November 12

Put on the new man which was created according to God,
in true righteousness and holiness.
EPHESIANS 4:24

In today's high-tech society, identity theft is a common occurrence. By obtaining the right personal information, one person can steal another's name, credit rating, and much more. It's a very real problem.

But, no one can rob you of your identity in Christ. When you seek God and put your trust in Him, He will transform your character and personality, developing within you qualities that no thief can steal. You are one of a kind; you cannot be duplicated.

Today, ask God to show you how to become more like Him. Let your identity come from who you are in Christ rather than from your material possessions, your looks, or what other people say about you.

God's Daily Answer

Do you know your identity in Christ? How has He transformed your life?

November 13

And we have known and believed the love
that God has for us. God is love, and he who
abides in love abides in God, and God in him.
1 JOHN 4:16

When we discover the love that only God can give, everything in life changes. He loves us so much that He is willing to accept us just the way we are—warts and all. His love covers all our shortcomings, and we do not have to earn the love that He so generously gives us. When we accept His offer to abide in His love, we abide in God and He is forever with us in every circumstance of life—and nothing or no one can take that away from us. Praise God!

—JACK COUNTRYMAN
Time with God for Mothers

Knowing that God is love, and that He abides in you, how can you show this trans-forming love to yourself and others?

_____

_____

_____

_____

_____

_____

_____

_____

November 14

In My Father's house are many mansions.

JOHN 14:2

Heaven is a big place! "In my Father's house are many mansions"—room enough for anyone and everyone who chooses to be a member of God's family! So please feel free to invite your entire family—including in-laws and out-laws, every one of your friends, all of your neighbors, the total population of your city, your state, your nation—everybody in the whole wide world!

—ANNE GRAHAM LOTZ
Heaven: My Father's House

What kind of a mansion has God planned for you?

November 15

*For by grace you have been saved through faith, and that not of
yourselves; it is the gift of God, not of works, lest anyone should boast.*
EPHESIANS 2:8–9

Most of what we receive in this life is deserved. We deserve a bonus at
our job because we worked hard, or we deserve a first-place finish in
a race because of all the grueling workouts we put in. We have a word for
things we receive but don't necessarily deserve: gifts. Christmas gifts, birthday gifts, unexpected gifts—they fall into the category of what the Bible calls
grace: things we receive that we don't earn. And when you add them up, the
list of God's gifts is long: love, forgiveness, and countless blessings. The Bible
tells us that God gives because He loves. That's the nature of grace: receiving without deserving. Pause for a second to thank God for the undeserved
blessings He has poured into your life—a moment to connect with the One
who has shown you grace is well worth the time.

—DAVID JEREMIAH
1 Minute a Day

Do you find it difficult to accept God's gifts because you feel undeserving?

_____

_____

_____

_____

_____

_____

_____

November 16

*Daniel answered and said: "Blessed be the name of God forever
and ever, for wisdom and might are His. And He changes the times
and the seasons; He removes kings and raises up kings; He gives wisdom
to the wise and knowledge to those who have understanding."*

DANIEL 2:20-21

We cannot understand God's wisdom unless we know, as He knows, the end from the beginning. And that's not possible. We see only the present through our own distorted angle, while God sees perfectly from everlasting to everlasting. "Behold, God is mighty . . . in strength of understanding" (Job 36:5).

The first nine chapters of Proverbs compel us to seek wisdom. "Wisdom is the principal thing; therefore get wisdom." (Proverbs 4:7). In Proverbs 8, "wisdom" may be regarded not as a mere personification of the attribute of wisdom, but as a divine person. "For whoever finds me finds life, and obtains favor from the LORD; but he who sins against me wrongs his own soul; all those who hate me love death" (Proverbs 8:35, 36). The apostle Paul declared "Christ the power of God and the wisdom of God" (1 Corinthians 1:24).

—JOHN HAGEE
Life Lessons to Live By

Are you seeking answers for your life—for your marriage, your finances, your children, your career? "Our Father" has the answer.

November 17

Love your enemies,
do good, . . . and your reward will be great.
LUKE 6:35

We may be tempted sometimes to conclude that because God doesn't fix our problem He doesn't love us. There are many things that He does not fix precisely because He loves us. Instead of extracting us from the problem, He calls us. In our sorrow or loneliness or pain He calls—"This is a necessary part of the journey. Even if it is the roughest part, it is only a part, and it will not last the whole long way. Remember where I am leading you. Remember what you will find at the end—a home and a haven and a heaven."

—ELISABETH ELLIOT
Keep a Quiet Heart

When you are asked to love your enemies, what is your first reaction?

November 18

Let your light so shine before men,
that they may see your good works and glorify
your Father in heaven.
MATTHEW 5:16

To the watching world, our lives paint a portrait of God. Our responses to times of gladness and sorrow are like paintbrushes sweeping across the canvas of life, leaving impressions of the God we call Savior. Through our actions and attitudes seekers gather information about this Jesus we proclaim.

With the help of the Holy Spirit, may our lives paint a picture of our God who is . . . patient but not passive . . . accepting but not pliable . . . holy but not untouchable . . . near but not us.

—ALICIA BRITT CHOLE
Pure Joy

What are some things that can come between you and God's light?

_____

_____

_____

_____

_____

_____

_____

_____

_____

November 19

*Be anxious for nothing, but in everything by prayer and
supplication, with thanksgiving, let your requests be made known
to God; and the peace of God which surpasses all understanding,
will guard your hearts and minds through Christ Jesus.*
PHILIPPIANS 4:6–7

But what about the circumstances in my life that are not blessings? What about my struggles, my grief, my loneliness, my pain, my past? How can I give thanks for those?

God knows that living in this world is not easy. He doesn't expect you to deny your problems or pretend all is well when it isn't. Instead, He longs for you to invite Him into your pain and then let genuine thanksgiving well up from a heart hidden in Him.

The Lord God is your refuge and strength . . . your present help in times of trouble. He is with you always and always faithful to His Word. As you thank Him for His presence and His promises, you open your heart to receive His peace . . . a supernatural peace that only comes to a heart that's confident in Him.

—KARLA DORNACHER
Give Thanks

Have you ever experienced this type of peace during the hard times in your life?

November 20

But Jesus looked at them and said to them, "With men this
is impossible, but with God all things are possible."
MATTHEW 19:26

S o many times in life we fail to realize that all things are possible through
God. He is the God of absolute possibilities. When you choose to honor
God, live for Him, and serve Him with all your heart, you can find true contentment. Psalm 37:4 says, "Delight yourself also in the LORD, and He shall
give you the desires of your heart." When you spend time with God and He
becomes an important part of your life, He places within your heart the desire to honor Him and bring glory to His Holy name. Praise God!

—JACK COUNTRYMAN
Time with God for Mothers

Not only does God accomplish things that may seem to us physically impossible, but
also spiritually impossible. What are some examples of times in your life, physical or
spiritual, when you have seen God overcome the impossible? What impossibility are
you currently facing?

November 21

Now therefore,
Arise, O Lord God, to Your resting place,
You and the ark of Your strength.
2 CHRONICLES 6:41

The spiritual warfare that Satan wages for your soul begins in your mind. Thus Paul says that we are to "take the helmet of salvation" (Ephesians 6:17), for the helmet protects the head.

You are wounded in your head when you are controlled by conditions such as depression, anger, and fear. You are wounded in your head when your thoughts are negative and suspicious and your imaginations are vulgar and sensual. That's why 2 Corinthians 10:5 says, "Casting down arguments and every high thing that exalts itself against the knowledge of God, bringing every thought into captivity to the obedience of Christ." When you find yourself thinking about something that is not of God, put on the helmet of your salvation in Christ, which brings renewal and wholeness.

—JOHN HAGEE
Life Lessons to Live By

Do you see your salvation only as a means of getting into heaven? Or do you see from God's Word that it is also a means to protect you in spiritual warfare and the power and hope to live a more abundant life?

November 22

Respecting the LORD *and not being proud*
will bring you wealth, honor, and life.
PROVERBS 22:4 NCV

Do you have a healthy, fearful respect for God's power? If so, you are both wise and obedient. God praises humility and punishes pride. That's why God's greatest servants will always be those humble men and women who care less for their own glory and more for God's glory. In God's kingdom, the only way to achieve greatness is to shun it. And the only way to be wise is to understand these facts: God is great; He is all-knowing; and He is all-powerful. We must respect Him, and we must humbly obey His commandments, or we must accept the consequences of our misplaced pride.

—CRISWELL FREEMAN
Purpose for Everyday Living

Find two verses from the Bible that address humility and pride and write them below. Pray that the motives of your heart will be to glorify God in all that you do.

November 23

Cast your burden on the LORD,
And He shall sustain you;
He shall never permit the righteous to be moved.
PSALM 55:22

When David wrote this psalm, he penned for you an outline of God's desire for you. The Lord wants very much for you to cast all of your burdens upon Him. He is willing and He is able to sustain you in every circumstance of life. When you love and worship the Lord, He will enable you to handle anything that may come against you. He will never run out of mercy, love, or grace.

—JACK COUNTRYMAN
Time with God for Mothers

Have you ever felt so overwhelmed that you just want to get away, to escape? Why don't you cast your burdens upon Jesus and escape into His arms.

November 24

*The LORD will guide you always; he will satisfy your needs in a
sun-scorched land and will strengthen your frame. You will be like
a well-watered garden, like a spring whose waters never fail.*
ISAIAH 58:11 NIV

I will satisfy your needs in a sun-scorched land and will strengthen your
frame. I have perfect knowledge of your body's condition. *Your frame was
not hidden from Me when you were made in secret.* I handcrafted you Myself;
you are *fearfully and wonderfully made!*

I am the Gardener, and you are My garden. Even when you are enduring
sun-scorching trials I can *satisfy your needs* and keep you *well watered, like a
spring whose waters never fail.* To receive My unfailing provisions, you need
to trust Me and thank Me—no matter what.

I, your sovereign Lord, *will guide you always.* I delight in watching over
you and helping you walk in My ways. Remember, though, that you also
have responsibility: to follow the guidance I provide. It is essential to study
My Word, for I am vibrantly present in it. The closer you live to Me, the easier it is to find and follow My path for you. This way of living is not only for
guidance but also for matchless enjoyment. *I will show you the path of Life; in
My Presence is fullness of Joy; at My right hand are pleasures forevermore.*

—SARAH YOUNG
Jesus Lives

List some ways that the Lord satisfies your needs—and thank Him for them.

_____

_____

_____

_____

November 25

We, according to His promise,
look for new heavens and a new earth in
which righteousness dwells.
2 PETER 3:13

If God could make the heavens and earth as beautiful as we think they are today—which includes thousands of years of wear and tear, corruption and pollution, sin and selfishness—can you imagine what the new heaven and the new earth will look like?

—ANNE GRAHAM LOTZ
Heaven: My Father's House

What comes to mind when you think of a new heaven and a new earth?

November 26

Every man did what was right in his own eyes.
JUDGES 17:6 NASB

In the book, *The Day America Told the Truth*, Patterson and Kim found that in every region of the country 90% of the people believe in God. But when they asked them how they made up their mind on issues of right and wrong, they found people do not turn to God or religion to help them decide about moral issues of the day. They concluded, "There is absolutely no moral consensus at all."

In other words, people believe there is a God, but He has no relevance to their everyday life yet. True belief in God is about trust and obedience. We trust Him to know and want the best for us, so we obey His command and His word. It's radically counter-cultural, but it's the best way to live.

Having Jesus as Lord means loving God enough to trust and obey Him, and loving your neighbor as yourself. It connects God with morality in a way that is good for all.

—BRYANT WRIGHT
Right from the Heart

How has knowing Jesus as Lord changed you morally?

I know that you can do all things
and that no plan of yours can be ruined. . . .
I talked of things too wonderful for me to know. . . .
My ears had heard of you before,
but now my eyes have seen you.
JOB 42:2–3, 5 NCV

Job desperately needed to know God's presence. If only God would make himself plainly known, Job would have something to count on, something to keep his hope alive. And, toward the end of the story, God finally appeared to Job in all his sovereign power and glory. And, after hearing from the Lord a thunderous barrage of unanswerable questions, Job admitted that he had talked about things that he did not understand and that he had spoken of things too wonderful for him to know. Job never received an answer to his first question—"Why?" But Job did gain the new understanding that his only hope was in God.

—SHEILA WALSH
Good Morning, Lord

What "why?" in your life are you willing to let go of as an act of hope, an act done in light of the fact that your destiny is interwoven with God's sovereign power and will for your life?

November 28

My sheep hear My voice, and I know them, and they follow Me.
JOHN 10:27

God's Spirit wishes to speak to your spirit, if you will but take the time to listen to the sound of His voice. He has promised to sustain you and give you eternal life. There is nothing or no one that can take that away from you. You belong to God, and He wants very much to be involved in every area of your life—to guide you, comfort you, sustain you, and give you the peace that passes all understanding. What a wonderful Savior is Jesus our Lord!

—JACK COUNTRYMAN
Time with God for Mothers

Do you allow yourself to be led as a sheep by the Great Shepherd of your soul, who wants to lead you by still waters?

November 29

All of you be submissive to one another, and be clothed with humility, for
"God resists the proud,
But gives grace to the humble."
1 PETER 5:5 NKJV

Some think being humble means being weak. But that's simply not the case. True humility is a character trait of God. He has plenty of reason to exalt His accomplishments and remind us of how powerful He is. After all, He created the universe and everything in it. But instead, He focuses on His children—loving, caring for, and encouraging them.

Ask God to help you always exhibit true humility. Go about your business, doing what God has called you to do and remembering that He is your Helper. The Bible says that the day will come when He will exalt you.

God's Daily Answer

Most times it takes more strength to throw off your pride and become humble. Can you think of a time when you felt stronger after humbling yourself?

_____

_____

_____

_____

_____

_____

_____

_____

_____

November 30

I am the way, the truth, and the life.
No one comes to the Father except through Me.
JOHN 14:6

Oprah Winfrey has been called the high priestess of afternoon comfort. Because of her amazing ability to connect with her viewers and to make them feel good about themselves, she has become the most influential spokesman of American spirituality today. Listen to what she says, "One of the biggest mistakes humans can make is to believe that there is only one way. Actually, there are many diverse paths leading to what you call God."

Chuck Colson says, "The Church of O encourages people to ask all the right questions about life … and then looks in precisely the wrong place to find those answers, which is within." The Bible shows us the one true path to God and that is through Jesus Christ. Jesus says that no one is going to get to heaven; no one is going to get to God, except through Him.

—BRYANT WRIGHT
Right from the Heart

Do you believe that Jesus is the only way to heaven? What do you say when someone asks you about finding their way to heaven?

_____

_____

_____

_____

_____

_____

_____

December

God's love is a sun that never sets.
ARTHUR JOHN GOSSIP

December 1

*And take the . . . word of God; praying always with all prayer
and supplication in the Spirit, being watchful to this end
with all perseverance and supplication for all the saints.*
EPHESIANS 6:17–18

Prayer is a powerful weapon of attack in spiritual warfare. Prayer has no limitations. Prayer can pull down every demonic stronghold in your city, crush the gates of hell, and conquer disease. But a prayerless Christian is a powerless Christian.

In Acts 12:1–6, Peter was held in prison and scheduled for execution. "But constant prayer was offered to God for him by the church" (v. 5). They had an all-night prayer meeting. And heaven's response? God miraculously delivered Peter.

When you begin to pray, believe that angels are released to help you through prayer.

—JOHN HAGEE
Life Lessons to Live By

Read Daniel 10:12–19. Now list anything happening in your life that you haven't prayed about. Then . . . pray! Pray with all belief that God hears your prayers and will strengthen you and help you.

_____

_____

_____

_____

_____

_____

December 2

The LORD says, "I will make you wise and show you where to go.
I will guide you and watch over you."
PSALM 32:8 NCV

From time to time, all of us encounter circumstances that test our faith. When we encounter life's inevitable tragedies, trials, and disappointments, we may be tempted to blame God or to rebel against Him. But the trials of life have much to teach us, and so does God.

Have you recently encountered one of life's inevitable tests? If so, remember that God still has lessons that He intends to teach you.

—CRISWELL FREEMAN
Purpose for Everyday Living

What "lesson" is God trying to teach you today?

December 3

Let him who thinks he stands take heed lest he fall.
1 CORINTHIANS 10:12

Victory is indeed a fleeting experience—and that may be especially true of spiritual victories.

You may have held your tongue (victory), but it won't be long before another rude comment comes your way (temptation). Or you may have controlled your temper (victory), but the next spark could soon ignite a rage (temptation). Thinking about how well you did in a given situation—as opposed to giving thanks for the Spirit's help—makes you prideful and an easy target for failure.

While you're busy celebrating success, the enemy can catch you off guard and bring you plummeting down. So praise *God* for your success. Focusing on Him like that will keep you from letting pride suggest that you're invincible.

—HENRY AND RICHARD BLACKABY
Discovering God's Daily Agenda

What areas of your life are easy targets for the enemy? Be ready to focus on praising God the next time you experience spiritual victory.

December 4

But the Lord is the true God;
He is the living God and the everlasting King.
JEREMIAH 10:10

Looking down over the battlements of heaven God saw this planet swinging in space—doomed, damned, crushed, and bound for hell. He saw you and me struggling beneath our load of sin. He made His decision.

The angelic hosts bowed in humility and awe as heaven's Lord of lords, who could speak worlds into space, got into His jeweled chariot, went back through the pearly gates, across the steep of the skies, and on a black Judean night, while the stars sang together and the escorting angels chanted His praise, stepped out of the chariot, threw off His robes, and became man!

—BILLY GRAHAM
Peace with God

When the Bible speaks of God's wrath, what do you envision?

December 5

Many plans are in a man's heart,
But the counsel of the LORD will stand.
PROVERBS 19:21 NASB

What on earth am I here for? Have you ever asked yourself, "What on earth am I here for?" Rick Warren asks that question in *The Purpose Driven Life*.

It seems the average American thinks life is all about working hard, raising a family, doing your best, making enough money to retire (the earlier the better), and then finally doing what you want to do when you want to do it. But by mid-life, this philosophy makes a person cry, "What on earth am I here for?" It's like slowly drowning in an ocean of emptiness.

But I have good news. We can know what on earth we're here for. It begins when we get to know our Creator through the person of Christ. Our Creator, God, loves us and has a purpose for our life. And our role is to trust Him and obey Him through His written word.

So don't waste your life. Get to know your Creator personally. I promise you'll become clear about what on earth you're here for.

—BRYANT WRIGHT
Right from the Heart

Are you clear on your life purpose? Can you write it down?

_____

_____

_____

_____

_____

December 6

The LORD leads with unfailing love and faithfulness all
who keep his covenant and obey his demands.
PSALM 25:10 NLT

The spiritual gift of giving is developed by our willingness to do what God's Word says, and to hear and respond to the voice of the Holy Spirit leading us. But sometimes in giving, if you wait, Satan is given time to come up with all kinds of good reasons not to do what God has told you to do. The longer you wait, the more time there is for your mind and emotions to cloud the message.

Don't give Satan an opportunity to help you rationalize another course of action. If God speaks, do it. Trust and obey, and watch miracles begin to happen in your finances.

—ROBERT MORRIS
The Blessed Life

Can you think of a time when God recently tested you regarding your finances? What was the outcome?

_____

_____

_____

_____

_____

_____

_____

_____

December 7

*And God will wipe away every tear from their eyes;
there shall be no more death, nor sorrow, nor crying. There
shall be no more pain, for the former things have passed away.*

REVELATION 21:4

What a wonderful promise God has given each of us. We can look forward to being with our Lord and Savior, and we can celebrate His love which is everlasting. Whatever trials we face or whatever seemingly impossible problems we encounter, God assures us that we can trust in His goodness and grace. Therefore, let us rejoice in all of our circumstances and praise God for the gift of a new life in Him, which He has generously given us.

—JACK COUNTRYMAN
Time with God for Mothers

Does God's promise to finally wipe away all of your tears one day give you hope and strength to live through your trials today?

December 8

*Lord, you bless those who do what is right;
you protect them like a solder's shield.*
PSALM 5:12 NCV

Are you often afraid? Today's world can be a scary place. It seems as though every day brings news of terrorist attacks, street rioting, or school violence.

But you must not live your life behind locked doors, either physically or mentally. Instead, trust in God, who promises to provide security to those who call on His name—to make you feel safe even in troubled times. Listen for the quiet, still voice of God alerting you to take shelter in Him when danger is near. Let Him be your armor and shield.

God's Daily Answer

Do you rest securely in God's protection each and every day as you continue to live your life for Him?

December 9

Because of the LORD's great love we are not consumed, for his compassions never fail. They are new every morning; great is your faithfulness. I say to myself, "The LORD is my portion; therefore I will wait for him."
LAMENTATIONS 3:22–24

My compassions never fail; they are new every morning. You can begin each day confidently, knowing that My vast reservoir of blessings is full—to the brim. This knowledge helps you *wait for Me*, entrusting your long-unanswered prayers into My care and keeping. I assure you that not one of your prayers has slipped past Me, unnoticed.

Although many of your prayers remain unanswered, you can trust in *My great faithfulness:* I keep all My promises in My perfect way and timing. Among other things, I have promised to *give you Peace* that displaces the trouble and fear in your heart.

If you become weary of waiting for answers to your prayers, remember that I also wait: so that *I may be gracious to you* and *have mercy on you.* I wait till you are ready to receive the things I have lovingly prepared for you. *Blessed are all those who wait for Me*—expectantly, longingly, trustingly.

—SARAH YOUNG
Jesus Lives

Why do loving parents sometimes make their children wait? How might God be working in you and your current situation as you wait?

_____

_____

_____

_____

December 10

The LORD is my shepherd;
I shall not want.
PSALM 23:1

One name that reveals the character and purpose of God is *Jehovah-Rohi*, "The Lord My Shepherd." Because He is my Shepherd, I shall not want for joy because in His presence is the fullness of joy. I shall not want for peace because He is the Prince of peace. I shall not want for rest because He makes me to lie down in green pastures. I shall not want forgiveness because He restores my soul. I shall not want prosperity because He prepares a table before me in the presence of my enemies. His goodness gives me what I do not deserve, and His mercy spares me from what I do deserve. God is watching me, and He knows exactly what I need. He knows exactly where to take me to get what satisfies my soul.

—JOHN HAGEE
Life Lessons to Live By

Do you want for joy, peace, rest, or forgiveness? Do you think you lack these because you have yet to give up control? Why not hand your life over to your Shepherd and let Him give you these things.

December 11

*Do not love the world or the things in the world. If anyone
loves the word, the love of the Father is not in him.*
1 JOHN 2:15

We live in the world, but we must not worship it. Our duty is to place God first and everything else second. But because we are fallible beings with imperfect faith, placing God in His rightful place is often difficult. In fact, at every turn, or so it seems, we are tempted to do otherwise. The world seems to cry, "Worship me with your time, your money, your energy, and your thoughts!" But God commands otherwise: He commands us to worship Him and Him alone.

—CRISWELL FREEMAN
Purpose for Everyday Living

List any ways you struggle with loving the things of this world more than you should. Pray for God's help in turning your focus back to Him.

December 12

Now thanks be to God who always leads us in triumph in Christ.
2 CORINTHIANS 2:14

George Patton said there are three elements to military victory: attack, attack, attack. And he was exactly right. Paul said it this way: "Pulling down strongholds" (2 Corinthians 10:4).

You attack the enemy through prayer and fasting, through prayer and evangelism, through the confession of the Word of God. If you are going through a problem, find every verse in the Bible about that kind of problem and write them down. Read them over and over and recite them aloud.

Remember that Jesus said, "All authority has been given to Me in heaven and on earth" (Matthew 28:18). He has all spiritual authority, and we are to use it over the kingdom of darkness. Christ shares His power and triumph with us!

—JOHN HAGEE
Life Lessons to Live By

How often do you come to the throne of Grace and ask God to give you the wisdom to attack the enemy?

December 13

The LORD is my rock and my fortress and my deliverer;
My God, my strength, in whom I will trust;
My shield and the horn of my salvation, my stronghold.
PSALM 18:2

From what do you need to be delivered? Perhaps you are weighed down by events in your past. Are you imprisoned by unforgiveness? Do recurring habits plague you and keep you from being the man or woman you want to be? Does shame—that internal tape telling you that you are hopelessly flawed and not worth loving—haunt you? Do you ever question the purpose of your life? Is fear a constant companion? Are you lonely? Are you feeling a degree of hopelessness? Whatever situation, emotion, or thought has its claws in you, I believe that God can deliver you!

—SHEILA WALSH
Good Morning, Lord

Put down in black and white those things from which you need to be delivered.

December 14

*Those who are wise shall shine
like the brightness of the firmament.*
DANIEL 12:3

I am amazed to see, how frequently the giving of gifts is mentioned in the Bible. . . . Rebekah accepts gifts of jewelry and clothing, symbolic of her acceptance of Isaac as her husband. Jacob tries to give a lavish present of livestock to the brother he has wronged. . . . Wise Men bring gifts to an Infant—gold, which acknowledges their King, frankincense their God, myrrh their Redeemer.

—CATHERINE MARSHALL
Moments that Matter

What steps can you take to become spiritually wise?

December 15

The joy of the LORD will make you strong.
NEHEMIAH 8:10 NCV

When your heart is full of joy, it spills over into every other area of your life. It makes hard tasks appear easier, aggravating situations seem less annoying, and disappointment feel less devastating. In short, it gives you the strength to face tough times. And it just makes life more fun.

Joy goes deeper than circumstance. It isn't dependent upon you winning the lottery or even being able to squeeze in your favorite activity. True joy, the kind that doesn't disappear when times get hard, is dependent on one thing—God's presence in your life. Knowing God is near and that He promises to bring good out of every circumstance in your life is a source of joy that will never run dry.

God's Daily Answer

Our moods can change as life happens, but does your attitude toward life depend upon circumstance or upon God's promise that He would never leave your side?

December 16

If anyone serves Me, let him follow Me.
JOHN 12:26

God deals differently with each of us. He knows no "typical" case. He seeks us out at a point in our own need and longing and runs down the road to meet us. This individualized treatment should delight rather than confuse us, because it so clearly reveals the highly personal quality of God's love and concern.

—CATHERINE MARSHALL
Moments that Matter

If Jesus were to ask you whom do you serve, what would you say?

_____

_____

_____

_____

_____

_____

_____

_____

_____

_____

_____

_____

_____

December 17

No temptation has overtaken you except such as is common to man; but God is faithful, who will not allow you to be tempted beyond what you are able, but with the temptation will also make the way of escape, that you may be able to bear it.

1 CORINTHIANS 10:13

The Word of God is your protection from Satan when he attacks your mind, your marriage, or your ministry. When Satan tempted Jesus in the wilderness, Jesus answered him with the Word of God. Satan quoted the Word of God back to Jesus, twisting the Scripture and trying to get Jesus to destroy Himself (Matthew 4:6). If Satan twisted Scripture with Jesus, he will do so with you.

When Satan whispers, "You're defeated," you need to shout back the words of Scripture, "We are more than conquerors through Him who loved us" (Romans 8:37). When Satan attacks your mind with fear, you need to fight back with a word that says, "For God has not given us a spirit of fear, but of power and of love and of a sound mind" (2 Timothy 1:7). Counterattacks with exactly what the Word of God says. That is the liberating power of the Word of God!

—JOHN HAGEE
Life Lessons to Live By

Are you familiar enough with God's Word and His promises to use them to defend yourself from Satan's attacks as Jesus did?

December 18

Those who sow in tears
Shall reap in joy.
PSALM 126:5

God does not waste our tears. He counts and invests each one. Tears of brokenness water the dry and parched places in our souls and in our world.

One more ingredient is essential though if our tears are to produce fruit: sowing.

In the midst of pain, we are to give. In the midst of heartache, we are to serve.

Brokenness – service = bitterness
Brokenness + service = fruitfulness

—ALICIA BRITT CHOLE
Pure Joy

When has your brokenness caused you to come to Christ?

December 19

The Son of Man will come in the glory
of His Father with His angels, and then He will
reward each according to his works.

MATTHEW 16:27

If with courage and joy we pour ourselves out for God and for others for His sake, it is not possible to lose, in any final sense, anything worth keeping. We will lose ourselves and our selfishness. We will gain everything worth having.

—ELISABETH ELLIOT
Keep a Quiet Heart

What type of reward will you receive for your works?

_____

_____

_____

_____

_____

_____

_____

_____

_____

_____

_____

_____

December 20

I will instruct you and teach you
in the way you should go;
I will guide you with My eye.
PSALM 32:8

One of the secrets of life is to always remain teachable. Growing in Jesus Christ is a process that God has promised to lead us through when we open our hearts and seek His guidance daily. God wants us to know Him, and He has promised to teach each of us in the way we should go. Isaiah 30:21 says, "This *is* the way, walk in it." Let each day be filled with the power of God's Spirit, that He might give wisdom and understanding, so that our lives may be everything God has planned.

—JACK COUNTRYMAN
Time with God for Mothers

Do you think that you have "arrived" in life, and that there is nothing left to learn? Or do you open your heart to God and seek His guidance daily?

December 21

But Noah found grace in the eyes of the LORD.
GENESIS 6:8

Noah surely felt strengthened as he walked with God and lived in His favor. How else could he have started such an outrageous project as building a huge boat in a desert nation where it seldom rained—when he was six hundred years old? Picture an old man struggling to coat the giant vessel inside and out with tar while his neighbors stood around the ladder, laughing and criticizing him. And then picture God holding the ladder steady and shouting up encouragement only Noah could hear: "That's it, Noah. Good job, son!"

In the same way, God's grace empowers us to do everyday acts of kindness and outrageous acts of courage on His behalf. Step out confidently on the path God sets before you, no matter how outrageous the goal may seem at the time. The God who steadied the ladder for Noah will hold you steady as you do His work today.

—BARBARA JOHNSON
Women of Faith Devotional Bible

Has God asked you to do something that others thought was outrageous, but you knew He was leading and helping you every step of the way?

December 22

Happy are the people whose
God is the Lord!
PSALM 144:15

We are God's treasure! When God the Father looked throughout the universe for something to give His only Son in reward for what He had accomplished on earth, the Father handpicked you! You are the Father's priceless gift of love to the Son!

—ANNE GRAHAM LOTZ
Heaven: My Father's House

How do you feel about being the Father's priceless gift of love?

December 23

*When Jesus spoke again to the people, he said, 'I am the
light of the world. Whoever follows me will never
walk in darkness, but will have the light of life.'*
JOHN 8:12

My wife Anne and I often ride through nearby neighborhoods, enjoying
the Christmas lights. Ever so often we'll come across a truly awesome
display covering the house and yard and trees, and Anne will say, "Now that
really is over the top there!" And I'll say, "Yeah, bless their heart." (That's a
Southern gentleman's way of saying, "You know it really is *pitiful* looking,
isn't it?") But whatever the case, I've got good news for you if you're one
of those that have all those lights. You see, lights are an important symbol
of the meaning of Christmas. Jesus entered this world to be the light in the
darkness, and God got in on the original light show. After all, the angels appeared to the shepherds, and whenever angels appear they often have this
dazzling array around them. And then there was the star over Bethlehem
that the wise men were drawn to.

So the next time you go driving around looking at Christmas lights, remember the coming of Jesus, "the Light of the world."

—BRYANT WRIGHT
Right from the Heart

We are called to be a light to the world. In what ways do you let your light shine?

December 24

The fear of man brings a snare,
But whoever trusts in the Lord shall be safe.
PROVERBS 29:25

As we consider the uncertainties of the future, we are confronted with a powerful temptation: the temptation to "play it safe." Unwilling to move mountains, we fret over the molehills. Unwilling to entertain great hopes of tomorrow, we focus on the unfairness of the today.

Ask God for the courage to step beyond the boundaries of your doubts. Ask Him to guide you to a place where you can realize your full potential—a place where you are freed from fear of failure. Don't ask Him to lead you to a "safe" place; ask him to lead you to the "right" place, and remember, those two places are seldom the same.

—CRISWELL FREEMAN
Purpose for Everyday Living

What are some ways you tend to "play it safe" instead of taking steps toward realizing your full potential?

December 25

They shall obtain joy and gladness,
And sorrow and sighing shall flee away.
ISAIAH 35:10

The black, velvety sky was clear and studded with sparkling stars that had looked down on Earth since the beginning of time. On the clear night air, sound traveled easily and somewhere from the direction of the village inn someone slammed a door.

The Seed of the woman, who would open heaven's gate and welcome any and all who place their faith in Him . . . had been given!

The Hope that was born that night continues to radiate down through the years until it envelops your heart and mine.

—ANNE GRAHAM LOTZ
God's Story

What do you want to share this Christmas that will bring joy to someone's heart?

_____

_____

_____

_____

_____

_____

_____

_____

_____

_____

December 26

Peace I leave with you, My peace I give to you;
not as the world gives do I give to you.
JOHN 14:27

Jesus didn't leave a material inheritance to His disciples. All He had when He died was a robe, which went to the Roman soldiers; His mother, whom He turned over to His brother John; His body, which He gave to Joseph of Arimathea; and His Spirit, which returned to His Father.

But Jesus willed His followers something more valuable than gold, more enduring than vast landholdings and more to be desired than palaces of marble—He willed us His peace.

—BILLY GRAHAM
The Secret of Happiness

Have you ever experienced the peace that passes all understanding?

December 27

The street of the city was pure gold,
like transparent glass.
REVELATION 21:21

The Bible tells us that when we get to heaven all of our sins and flaws will fall away, and we will be like Jesus. With our unique personalities and characteristics, every single one of us is going to perfectly reflect the character of Christ. And as we walk on streets that reflect like mirrors, every step we take and every move we make is going to bring glory to Him.

—ANNE GRAHAM LOTZ
Heaven: My Father's House

When you think of heaven, what comes to mind?

_____

_____

_____

_____

_____

_____

_____

_____

_____

_____

_____

_____

December 28

For you were once darkness, but now you are
light in the Lord. Walk as children of light.
EPHESIANS 5:8

I want you to live close to Me, seeing things from My perspective more and more. *Walk as a child of Light,* for My radiance is all around you and also within you; it transforms you inside and out. Remember that *you were once darkness* until My Spirit quickened you to Life, empowering you to live in My holy Presence. Dwell on this blessed remembrance until gratitude for My *glorious grace* wells up within you.

Trust Me to lead you step by step through each day. I provide sufficient Light for only one day at a time. If you try to look into the future, you will find yourself peering into darkness: *My Face shines upon you* only in the present! This is where you find My gracious Love that never fails you. Live ever so near Me—flourishing in My transforming Light.

—SARAH YOUNG
Jesus Lives

What does it mean to "walk" as a "child" of "Light"? Prayerfully meditate on and
write about each of these key words in today's featured verse.

December 29

I am with you always,
even to the end of the age.
MATTHEW 28:20

Remember, Christ is always near us. We should say nothing that we would not wish to say in His Presence. We should do nothing that we would not do in His Presence. We should go no place that we would not go in His Presence. But He is not with us just to judge or condemn us; He is near to comfort, protect, guide, encourage, strengthen, and help.

—BILLY GRAHAM
The Secret of Happiness

Describe in your own words, the phrase, "I am with you always."

_____

_____

_____

_____

_____

_____

_____

_____

_____

_____

_____

_____

December 30

The LORD your God has chosen you to be a
people for Himself, a special treasure.
DEUTERONOMY 7:6

While traveling in the former Soviet Union and sharing God's "plan" of salvation with students, we never used the word *plan* since the Russians associated the word with the Communist Plan. We used, instead, the word *dream*, a close counterpart in their language. I remember talking with Svetlana, telling her God has a "dream" for her life. She lowered her beautiful face and asked shyly, "Does He know I am a Soviet citizen?" "Yes," I responded. "And still," she pondered, "He has a *dream* about my life?"

I assured her that indeed God has a purpose for those who belong to Him. His purpose is to love us intensely and lead us intentionally into a broad place where we can know and enjoy His faithfulness to us. His commitment toward us is full of promise.

—MARY GRAHAM
Women of Faith Devotional Bible

Do you believe that God has a dream and purpose for your life, or do you sometimes feel unworthy of God's love and mercy?

December 31

Wait on the LORD;
Be of good courage,
And He shall strengthen your heart;
Wait, I say, on the LORD!
PSALM 27:14

Waiting is not a very popular word in the life of most people in our culture. We want everything . . . *now*, but God has promised that He will act on our behalf when we wait for Him. Many times we choose not to wait; instead, we run ahead of Him and try to fix things on our own. If we will only wait on the Lord, He promises to strengthen our hearts and give us the courage to wait for His answers. Seek His strength today.

—JACK COUNTRYMAN
Time with God for Mothers

Waiting on God is a very tough concept, especially in our culture of deadlines and decisions. Have there been times when you waited faithfully on God and He came through? Do you still trust in Him to continue to come through for you?

_____

_____

_____

_____

_____

_____

_____

_____